Orange Line 3

Workbook Lösungen

von

Pauline Ashworth
Peter Bremke
Geraldine Greenhalgh
Oliver Grothues
Margaret Gutmann
Marion Horner
Mary Jo Rabe

Herausgeber: Frank Haß

Ernst Klett Verlag
Stuttgart • Leipzig

Mein Sprachenpass

Hast du das, was du auf Englisch schon kannst, auch in den Ferien verwenden können?
Nimm dir doch ein bisschen Zeit und fülle wieder deinen Sprachenpass aus.

Wo hast du in den Ferien etwas auf Englisch gehört oder gelesen?

____

Hast du auch Englisch gesprochen? Wenn ja, welche Wörter hast du besonders oft benutzt?

____

Hast du ein englisch-deutsches Wörterbuch benutzt?

____

Welches englische Lied gefällt dir besonders gut?

____

Welche englischen Internet-Seiten hast du dir angeschaut?

____

Wie lernst du am liebsten? Mit einem Partner oder mit dem Computer?
Durch Hören, Lesen, Schreiben oder Sprechen?

____

Welche Präsentationen und Projekte hast du in Englisch schon gemacht?

____

Jetzt kannst du wieder aufschreiben, welche Ziele du dir für das kommende Schuljahr im Fach Englisch vornehmen willst.

Das möchte ich in Englisch können:

____

____

Dafür werde ich folgendes tun:

____

Datum: ____________ Unterschrift: ______________________

Unit 1 What's your game?

1 Sports (→ p. 9/ex. 3)

Look at the pictures. Write down all the sports which you can find.

football, *hockey, basketball, volleyball, baseball, badminton, ice hockey, table-tennis, surfing*

2 Baseball (→ p. 9/ex. 3)

Find the correct order of the sentences a)–d).

Baseball is a team sport and it started in America. One player throws the ball, and another hits it with a bat and runs around the field.

a) Today kids play baseball at school and in clubs.
b) Babe Ruth[1], the most famous player of all times, made baseball even more popular in the 1920s.
c) By 1870 baseball was America's favourite sport, and there were many teams.
d) Jackie Robinson[2] became the first black player in 1947.

Everybody watches baseball on TV or in the stadiums. America loves baseball.

A baseball match in the 1920s.

c)	*b)*	*d)*	*a)*

3 More about baseball (→ p. 9/ex. 3) *(Lösungsvorschlag)*

Use the internet to answer the following questions.

1. Find out the names of two players from the Chicago Cubs. *Rocky Cherry, Michael Barret*
2. What's the name of a New York baseball team? *New York Jankees*
3. Find out the name of the number 1 player from the Cincinnati Reds. *Homer Bailey*

[1] Babe Ruth [beɪb ˈruːθ] – *amerikanischer Baseballspieler,* [2] Jackie Robinson [ˌdʒæki ˈrɒbɪnsn] – *amerikanischer Baseballspieler*

4 A sports star (→ p. 10/ex. 1)

Sally Smith is a famous baseball player. Read what she says about her life. Put in the correct forms of the simple present.

Baseball is *(be)* a great sport but it isn't *(not be)* easy. I practise *(practise)* every day and eat *(eat)* meat, vegetables and potatoes. Jenny, a girl in my team, never eats *(eat)* sweets because they aren't *(not be)* healthy. But I love *(love)* chocolate! Most of the other players in my team are *(be)* my friends and we have *(have)* a lot of fun. My mum thinks *(think)* I should have a boyfriend but I don't have *(not have)* enough time. Usually, I feel *(feel)* very excited before a match so I go *(go)* to bed very early. Sometimes I am *(be)* so nervous that I don't eat *(not eat)* anything. But every time we win *(win)* a match I feel *(feel)* like it's the best day of my life!

5 Wrong sentences (→ p. 10/ex. 1)

Read the exercise 'A sports star' again and correct these sentences.

1. Sally is a football player. Sally isn't a football player.
2. She practises three times a week. She practises every day.
3. Most of the players don't like Sally. Most of the players are her friends.
4. Jenny eats sweets every day. Jenny never eats sweets.
5. Before a match Sally goes to bed very late. Jenny goes to bed very early.
6. Usually, Sally feels very bored before a match. Jenny feels excited before a match.

6 A game: The simple present (→ p. 10/ex. 1) (individuelle Schülerlösung)

a) *Work with a partner. Make cards with the following words. Make sentences with the words on the cards. Be careful where you put the signal words!*

I	Derrek	we	don't	like	play	football	TV
you	they	Sally	doesn't	watch	eat	ice-cream	sport
						every day	often

Example: I | often | play | football

b) *Use your own words to make more cards.*

7 Flyball[1] (→ p. 10/ex. 2)

Flyball is a sport which dogs and people play together. Tony plays flyball with his dog Daisy every week. Read what he says and make questions.

1. *(How • you • play • flyball)* How do you play flyball?

   In flyball the dogs run a race against each other.

2. *(Where • dogs • run)* Where do the dogs run?

   The dogs run to a box and press a big button. Then a ball comes out of the box.

3. *(What • dog • do with the ball)* What does the dog do with the ball?

   The dog tries to catch the ball and brings it back to the owner.

4. *(you • have • teams)* Do you have teams?

   Yes, we have teams. Each team has four dogs.

5. *(you • practise • every day)* Do you practise every day?

   No, we practise every weekend.

6. *(Why • you • like • flyball)* Why do you like flyball?

   I like flyball because dogs and people work together as a team. And Daisy loves it, too!

8 Daisy's profile (→ p. 11/ex. 4)

Read Daisy's profile and write a short text about her.

Daisy

Daisy was born on 3rd May 2004. She was born in Southampton. Daisy is brown and white and her weight is 70 lb. She plays for the Four Fast Dogs. Tony Spencer is her owner.

Name:	Daisy
Date of birth:	03/05/2004
Place of birth:	Southampton
Colour:	brown and white
Weight:	70 lb
Team:	Four Fast Dogs
Owner:	Tony Spencer

9 A sports interview (→ p. 11/ex. 5) *(Lösungsvorschlag)*

Write down three questions about sport. Ask your partner these questions and write down his or her answers.

1. What is your favorite sport?
2. How often do you practise?
3. Which sport don't you like?

[1] flyball ['flaɪˌbɔːl] – *Flyball*

10 Crazy pictures (→ p. 12/ex. 1)

Can you find the four differences between the two pictures? Write sentences and use the present progressive.

The woman is eating a sandwich.	The woman is driking lemonade.
The girl is catching a ball.	The girl is throwing a ball.
The man is wearing a blue T-shirt.	The man is wearing a red T-shirt.
The boy is writing a text message.	The boy is sleeping.
The dog is barking.	The dog is eating a sausage.

11 What are you doing? (→ p. 12/ex. 2)

Marcia is talking to her friend Jenny on the phone. Jenny is asking Marcia what she is doing at the moment. Look at the pictures and write down Jenny's questions and Marcia's answers.

Jenny: Are you watching TV?

Marcia: No, I'm not watching TV.

Jenny: Are you listening to music?

Marcia: No, I'm not listening to music.

Jenny: Are you cleaning the living-room?

Marcia: No, I'm not cleaning the living-room.

Jenny: Is the cat running around?

Marcia: No, the cat isn't running around.

Jenny: Are the dogs barking?

Marcia: No, the dogs aren't barking.

Jenny: So what's that noise?!

Marcia: Oh, sorry, that's just my neighbour. He's singing under the shower.

watch

listen

clean

run around

bark

12 Signal words (→ p. 13/ex. 3)

There are signal words for the simle present and for the present progressive. Mark the signal words for the simple present in red and the words for the present progressive in blue.

right now | every year | always | now | today | at the moment | often | sometimes | just | usually

13 A strange day (→ p. 13/ex. 3)

a) *On Monday mornings Rob gets up at 8 o'clock. But something is wrong today. Look at the pictures and fill in the simple present or the present progressive.*

1. Something is wrong today. My parents usually have breakfast, but today they are sleeping.
2. My sister usually leaves the house at 9 o'clock, but today she is washing her hair.

3. Our cat usually catches the mice but today she is sitting on the sofa.
4. The dogs usually eat their food, but today they are running around.

b) *Look at the pictures again. Why is everything different today?* It's Sunday.

14 What are you doing? (→ p. 13/ex. 4)

Rob is chatting on the internet with his friend Charlie. Read the text and underline the signal words. Fill in the simple present or the present progressive.

Rob: What are you doing (*do*) at the moment?

Charlie: I 'm doing (*do*) my homework right now. I usually do (*do*) it after supper. What are you doing (*do*) at the moment?

Rob: At the moment I 'm working (*work*) on my website. I change (*change*) it sometimes. I 'm just putting in (*put in*) some new pictures.

Charlie: Oh brilliant! I always like (*like*) to see new pictures!

15 SKILLS: A sports survey (→ p. 14/ex. 1) *(individuelle Schülerlösung)*

a) *Do a survey in your class. Ask the pupils in your group which kinds of sport they watch on TV and how often they watch them. Collect the information and put it the grid.*

name	which sports?	how often?

b) *Look at the different kinds of sport. Collect pictures of all the sports in your group. Make a small poster and write down the names of the people from the grid who watch the sport next to the pictures.*

c) *Prepare a talk. Write notes about what you want to say.*

d) *Present it to the class.*

16 Let's listen: At the match (→ p. 15/ex. 2)

Listen to the dialogue and complete the sentences.

a) The fans from Australia have got kangaroos on their baseball caps.

Tess and Trina are sitting with a lot of England fans.

b) They are looking for Row F, seats thirty and thirty-one.

The seats are near the middle so they can see both goals.

c) The man tells Tess and Trina that they are sitting in Row E.

Tess and Trina are in the wrong row because part of the letter is missing.

d) Now, Tess and Trina need a cold drink!

17 Let's listen: Is it important to win? (→ p. 15/ex. 2)

a) *Listen to the dialogue. Why do people think it is or it is not important to win? Make notes in two lists.*

important to win	not important to win
you want to be the best	not everybody can win
you look like an idiot when you lose	it's silly to get fed up
it's much cooler to win	sport is for fun
everybody loves the person who wins	even when you lose you can enjoy it
when you win, it makes you happy	it's good to lose sometimes

b) *Check these phrases. Then listen again. Which of the phrases do you hear? Write a ✔ or a ✘.*

1. You're right. ✔
2. Yes, that's true. ✘
3. That's what I think, too. ✔
4. Sorry, but you're wrong. ✘
5. Don't be silly! ✔
6. I don't think that's true. ✔

18 Fair[1] play (→ p. 15/ex. 3) *(individuelle Schülerlösung)*

a) *Look at the pictures and describe what's happening. Write in your exercise book.* banana skin[2] tail[3]

b) *Do you think it's important to win? Why/why not? Discuss.*

[1] fair [feə] – *fair,* [2] banana skin [bəˌnaːnə 'skɪn] – *Bananenschale,* [3] tail [teɪl] – *Schwanz*

19 Mediation and communication: At a football match (→ p. 15/ex. 5)

You and your partner are at a football match in England with your friend. Your friend doesn't speak English. He asks you what the people are saying.

A	B

(Der Junge will zwei Tickets kaufen. Der Verkäufer fragt, ob er unter 16 ist. Der Junge sagt „ja". Der Verkäufer sagt, dass die Tickets dann zum halben Preis sind.
Der Junge fragt, wann das Spiel anfängt. Das Mädchen antwortet, dass das Spiel um viertel nach drei anfängt.
Der eine Mann fragt: „Hast du das gesehen?" Der andere antwortet: „Ja, das war toll!"
Die Fans sagen: „Hey, Schiedsrichter, das war ein Foul!" „Er hat den Torwart geschlagen!" „Oh nein, der Schiedsrichter verweist ihn vom Platz!"
Der eine Mann fragt nach dem Spielstand. Der andere Mann antwortet: „Zwei zu eins."
Der eine Junge sagt: „Tolles Spiel! Das Tor in den letzten fünf Minuten war toll!" Der andere Junge sagt: „Ja, das war fantastisch!")

20 A match to remember! (→ p. 17/ex. 3)

a) *Read this shorter form of the text 'A match to remember'. There are four parts to this story. Find the parts and mark them, each in a different colour.*

Last Wednesday Sarah came home with her friend Leo after football practice. But she couldn't find her key. "Oh, no! I've left my key in my other jacket." It was nearly five o'clock and her mum wasn't home yet. She and Leo sat down on the doorstep and Mr Barnes from next door saw them.
"Hello, Sarah," he said. Sarah didn't like him. He was really old and he never smiled. Every week he moaned to Sarah's mum about something. Sarah's cat dug up his plants or Sarah's music was too loud.
"He's a nice old man," said her mum. "He's just very lonely. I feel sorry for him." And sometimes she gave him a pot of jam. He invited Sarah and Leo to wait in his house until her mum came home.
"Would you like to wait in my house, Sarah? I can make you some hot chocolate." It was cold and wet on the doorstep so Sarah said "Thank you" and wrote a note for her mum.

Sarah's neighbour

In Mr Barnes's living room Leo saw an old photo of a football team.
"Where are you in this picture, Mr Barnes?" Leo asked.
"Oh, I didn't play for that team, Leo. That's Dynamo Moscow. I saw them in November 1945. They played against Arsenal at White Hart Lane. That was a match to remember."
"Why?" asked Sarah. She felt happier now.
"Well," said Mr Barnes. He smiled as he remembered:

An old photo

"One of the Arsenal players had a fight with one of the Russian players. The referee sent the Arsenal player off the field.
Suddenly a really thick fog came down. The referee couldn't see the pitch and the Arsenal player came back onto the pitch again."
"That wasn't fair," said Sarah. She laughed and Mr Barnes smiled again. He didn't look so old now.
"No," he said. "But the Russians had twelve players. They substituted one player but he came back. I think they had 15 players at the end of the match."
"What a laugh!" said Leo.
"But that wasn't all," said Mr Barnes. "The Arsenal goalkeeper ran into the goal post and knocked himself out."
"So Arsenal had one player fewer again," said Sarah. She couldn't stop laughing now.
"No!" said Mr Barnes. "A man from the crowd played in goal for the rest of the match."
"And was it a draw?" asked Leo.
"No," said Mr Barnes. "The Russians won. The score was four goals to three."

The match

Suddenly the doorbell rang. It was Sarah's mum.
"Thank you for the hot chocolate, Mr Barnes," said Leo.
"Yes, and for the funny story," added Sarah.

A new friend for Sarah

b) *Match these titles with the parts of the story. Write the titles next to the parts of the text.*

The match | A new friend of Sarah | Sarah's neighbour | An old photo

c) *What do Sarah and her mum talk about when they get home? What do you think? Write a short dialogue in your exercise book.* *(individuelle Schülerlösung)*

21 Word games (→ p. 18/ex. 1)

a) *Work with a partner. Put in the correct letters and see what word you get. Who's fastest?*

1. where you can play baseball
2. many times, more than once
3. tells the players what is right and wrong
4. you use it when you talk
5. not too little, not too much
6. in beach volleyball, you hit the ball over it
7. every game has Its own rules
8. a game with a ball; the players don't wear helmets

S	T	A	D	I	U	M
O	F	T	E	N		
U	M	P	I	R	E	
V	O	I	C	E		
E	N	O	U	G	H	
N	E	T				
I	T	S				
R	U	G	B	Y		

When you are away from home, you bring this back with you. souvenir

b) *Write your own crossword puzzle in your exercise book. Give it to your partner. Can he/she find all the answers?* (individuelle Schülerlösung)

22 Compare (→ p. 18/ex. 3)

Find the correct words.

1. Helmet is to American football as cap is to baseball.
2. Stadium is to football as court is to tennis.
3. Sand is to beach as grass is to field.
4. Umpire is to baseball as referee is to football.
5. Swimsuit is to pool as jersey is to bicycle.
6. Ball is to pitcher as whistle is to referee.
7. Back is to front as top is to bottom.

23 Do you like to play? (→ p. 19/ex. 5)

Write in the words for the rhymes.

1. I hit the ball and score a run. Baseball is a lot of fun.
2. Football helmets hurt my head. Can't I wear a cap instead?
3. I like the match but not the crowd. Why are they all so loud?
4. That's not rugby; that's a fight. Tell the players: That's not right!
5. I hit the ball across the net. But on the beach we all get wet.
6. The day is hot; that's really cool. Let's all swim in my new pool.

24 The first baseball game (→ p. 20/ex. 1)

Could this be the story of the first baseball game? Write in the correct verbs in the simple present.

throw | be | pick | throw | walk | watch | take | eat | come | hit | fly | have | catch | be

One day a boy watches his dad's sheep but the sheep are boring. They just walk around or eat.

There is an apple tree in the field. The boy picks up some apples and throws them at the sheep. The sheep run after the apples and the fastest sheep catches the apple. One day the boy throws a stick but the sheep don't run after it. So he takes a stick in one hand and an apple in the other hand. He throws the apple up. When it comes down he hits it with the stick. The ball flies far into the field and the sheep run after it. The boy has an idea for a new game.

25 What are they doing? (→ p. 21/ex. 3)

Look at the picture. What are the animals doing?

1. The cat is catching a bird.
2. The mice are eating cheese.
3. The tiger is climbing a tree.
4. The dog is playing with a ball.
5. The fish are swimming.
6. The birds are flying around.

26 What do you do? (→ p. 21/ex. 4)

What do you usually do and what are you doing today?

1. I usually do (*do*) my homework at 3 o'clock but today I 'm watching (*watch*) TV.
2. I usually walk (*walk*) in the park but today I 'm riding (*ride*) my bike.
3. I usually go (*go*) to bed at 8 o'clock but tonight I 'm going (*go*) to a party.
4. I usually take (*take*) my dog for a walk but today I 'm staying (*stay*) at home.
5. I usually work (*work*) in the garden but today I 'm not working (*not work*) there.
6. I usually eat (*eat*) apples, but today I 'm eating (*eat*) chocolate.

1 A recipe (→ p. 22/ex. 3)

a) *Read this recipe and underline all the words which you don't know.*

CHICAGO HOT DOG

- *1 sausage*
- *1 hot dog bun with poppy seeds*
- *½ onion (chopped)*
- *½ cup of yellow mustard*
- *½ cup of sweet pickle relish*
- *1 tomato (cut in wedges)*

Put water into a pot. Heat the water but don't let it boil! Add the sausage and cook for about 5 minutes until it is hot. Take out the sausage and put it into the bun. Top the hot dog with onion, mustard, tomato wedges and sweet pickle relish.

b) *Write down the English words which you have underlined in alphabetical order.*

English	German	English	German
bun	Brötchen	to cut	schneiden
poppy	Mohn	wedge	Keil
seed	Samen	pot	Topf
onion	Zwiebel	to heat	erhitzen
chopped	gehackt	to boil	kochen
mustard	Senf	to cook	kochen
pickle relish	eingelegtes Gemüse	to top	auffüllen

c) *Look up the words in your English-German dictionary. Write the German words next to the English words.*

d) *Tell your partner in German how to make a Chicago Hot Dog.*

2 Different meanings (→ p. 22/ex. 3)

What do these food names mean in German? Use your dicitionary and write down the German words.

1. pudding *Nachtisch*
2. mince *Hackfleisch*
3. stock *Brühe*
4. marmalade *Orangenmarmelade*

Meine Lernbiografie 1

Jetzt hast du die erste Unit bearbeitet und solltest wieder einmal über das Lernen nachdenken. Male zu jedem Satz einen Smiley in der entsprechenden Farbe. Wenn du dir nicht sicher bist, dann schau dir noch einmal die Übungen in der rechten Spalte an.

An welchen Stellen hast du „muss ich noch üben" ausgewählt? Nimm dir diese Bereiche in den nächsten Wochen noch einmal genau vor. Vielleicht schaffst du es, dort noch besser zu werden. Frage auch deinen Lehrer/deine Lehrerin, ob er/sie dir Tipps geben kann.

Was ich alles kann!

Trage den entsprechenden Smiley ein.

sehr gut | gut | muss ich noch üben

			Übung im ... Seite/Übung
Hören	Ich kann Hörtexten einzelne Informationen entnehmen und Fragen zum Gehörten beantworten.		Schülerbuch S. 9/2, 15/1, 2, 3 Workbook S. 9/16, 17
	Ich verstehe auch längere Hörtexte und kann Teile daraus wiedergeben.		Schülerbuch S. 15/2 c) Workbook S. 9/17 a)
Sprechen	Ich kann eine Person beschreiben.		Schülerbuch S. 11/4 Workbook S. 5/8
	Ich kann Angaben zu meiner eigenen Person machen.		Schülerbuch S. 11/5 Workbook S. 5/9
	Ich kann ein Thema präsentieren.		Schülerbuch S. 14/1 Workbook S. 8/15
	Ich kann erklären, wie eine Sportart gespielt wird.		Schülerbuch S. 9/3
	Ich kann über ein bestimmtes Thema diskutieren.		Workbook S. 9/18
	Ich kann eine Umfrage machen und präsentieren.		Workbook S. 8/15
	Ich kann ein Bild beschreiben.		Schülerbuch S. 13/6, 18/2, 21/3 Workbook S. 6/10, 13/25
	Ich kann mich über Sport und Urlaubs-erlebnisse/-Pläne unterhalten.		Schülerbuch S. 13/4, 5 Workbook S. 5/9
	Ich kann eine englische Unterhaltung auf Deutsch wiedergeben.		Workbook S. 10/19
	Ich kann Sätze im *simple present* bilden.		Schülerbuch S. 10/1, 2, 3 Workbook S. 4/4, 5, 6, S. 5/7
	Ich kann Sätze im *present progessive* bilden.		Schülerbuch S. 12/2, S. 13/5 Workbook S. 6/10, 11
	Ich kann das *simple present* vom *present progressive* unterscheiden.		Schülerbuch S. 12/2, S. 13/5 Workbook S. 6/10, 11

Lesen	Ich kann längere Geschichten lesen und verstehen.		Schülerbuch S. 17/3 Workbook S. 11/20
	Ich kann Einzelheiten aus Texten herausfinden und Aufgaben dazu lösen.		Schülerbuch S. 17/2, 4 Workbook S. 11/20
	Ich kann ein deutsch-englisches Wörterbuch benutzen.		Schülerbuch S. 22/1, 2, 3, 4, S. 23/5, 6, 7 Workbook S. 14/1, 2
Schreiben	Ich kann einen Steckbrief über mich selbst oder andere schreiben.		Schülerbuch S. 11/5, 6 Workbook S. 5/8
	Ich kann eine Pro- und Kontra-Tabelle ausfüllen.		Workbook S. 9/17 a)
	Ich kann einen kurzen Text über Erfundenes oder selbst Erlebtes schreiben.		Schülerbuch S. 17/4 Workbook S. 11/20

Was ich noch besser machen kann!

Nun hast du herausgefunden, was du besonders gut kannst und woran du noch arbeiten solltest. Dabei kann dir ein Lernplan helfen. Schreibe auf, welche Erfahrungen du beim Lernen gemacht hast und woran du in nächster Zeit arbeiten willst.

Welche Arbeiten aus deinem Folder zeigen besonders gut, was du erreicht hast und/oder wo du dich verbessert hast?

____

Welche Schwierigkeiten tauchten beim Lernen auf? Wie konntest du sie überwinden?

____

Worauf bist du in dieser Lerneinheit besonders stolz?

____

____

Was möchtest du in Zukunft noch stärker üben?

____

____

Tipps von deinem Lehrer/deiner Lehrerin:

____

____

Datum: ____________ Unterschrift: ________________________

Unit 2 Out and about in London

1 Pictures of London (→ p. 27/ex. 3)

Look at the pictures. What do they show? Write one sentence for each photo.

1

2

3

4

1. *Tube trains are much faster than buses.*
2. *Buckingham Palace is the home of the Royal Familiy.*
3. *You get spectacular views from the London Eye.*
4. *You can see the Crown Jewels in the Tower.*

2 London tips for young people (→ p. 27/ex. 3)

a) *Look at the tips for young people and answer the questions.*

London
Insider tips for young people

Tip 1: Cutty Sark
Learn about the history of the ship – and enjoy the ghost stories!
UNDERGROUND Camden Town

Tip 2: Tower Bridge
Walk across the high part of the bridge and see the fantastic views! Find out how the bridge opens for tall ships.
UNDERGROUND Tower Hill

Tip 3: The London Dungeon
If you like scary museums, you will love the London Dungeon. But be careful, some of the figures can move!
UNDERGROUND London Bridge

Tip 4: London's Transport Museum.
London's buses, trains and much more – from 1820 until today. The Museum shop is famous for its posters and souvenirs.
UNDERGROUND St. Paul's

1. What can you learn about at the Cutty Sark? *You can learn about the history of the ship.*
2. Where can you see fantastic views? *You can see fantastic views from Tower Bridge.*
3. Which London museum is scary? *The London Dungeon is scary.*
4. What does the Transport Museum show? *It shows London's buses and trains.*

b) *Look at the tips again. Where would you go first? Where wouldn't you like to go and why? Write in your exercise book.* *(individuelle Schülerlösung)*

3 The pickpocket is sorry (→ p. 28/ex. 1)

The pickpocket is now at the police station. Read the text and put in the correct forms.

was • wasn't • were • weren't

Policeman: Were ______ you on your way to school when you stole the jacket?

Pickpocket: No, I wasn't ______. I was ______ in town. I was ______ scared because there were ______ some bullies at school yesterday. They wanted money from me. It was ______ horrible. I was ______ really scared.

Policeman: But you weren't ______ too scared to steal all these things from those people.

Pickpocket: I was ______ more scared of the bullies. But now I can tell you everything. I'm really sorry!

4 Why did you do that? (→ p. 28/ex. 1)

The people want to know why the pickpocket stole their things. Find the correct phrases and make simple past forms.

think it is a real camera

think there is money in it ✓

want to give it to the bullies

not use any of them

1. Why did you steal my jacket? – I thought there was money in it.
2. Did you use any of my lip balms? – No, I didn't use any of them.
3. What did you want to do with the money? – I wanted to give it to the bullies.
4. Didn't you see that it was a toy camera? – No, I thought it was a real camera.

5 The way to St James's Park (→ p. 28/ex. 1)

The policeman told the pickpocket the way to St James's Park where he had to collect rubbish. Read what he said and write down the pickpocket's way.

> *Go* down the road. In five minutes you'll *come* to a Tube station. *Take* the Circle Line west and *get* off at St James's Park. When you *leave* the station you'll *see* the park. You'll *find* a lot of rubbish there.

The pickpocket went down the road. After five minutes he came to a Tube station. He took the Circle Line west and got off at St James's Park. When he left the station, he saw the park. He found a lot of rubbish there.

6 A new film star[1] (→ p. 28/ex. 1)

Stella Black is England's new film star. Her first action film 'Lions on a plane' came into the cinemas last week. Stella came to London for an interview. Read what she told the reporter. What questions did the reporter ask her?

1. My first role was in a school play. – Where?
2. My first role was the lion in *The Wizard of Oz*. – What?
3. Last year I tried to get a role in a film. – When?
4. I chose *Lions on a plane* because I love action films. – Why?

1. Where was your first role?
2. What was your first role?
3. When did you try to get a role in a film?
4. Why did you choose "Lions on a plane"?

7 Stella's day in London (→ p. 28/ex. 1)

After the interview Stella spent the rest of the day in London. Look at the pictures. What did she do? Write five sentences in the simple past and use a different verb in each sentence.

1. She bought a skirt at Harrods.
2. She ate pizza at the Pizza Oven.
3. She read a book about the Tower of London.
4. She went to the London Dungeon.
5. She took a tube train to Tower Hill.

8 Stella at Harrods (→ p. 29/ex. 2)

Stella hates skirts but she needs one for an important interview. What does she say to the shop assistant?

cheaper	black	smaller✓	trendier	+	one • ones

1. This skirt is too big. I think I need a smaller one.
2. I don't like the colour of this skirt. I'd like a black one.
3. I look like my grandma in this skirt. Please give me a trendier one.
4. This skirt is a bit too expensive. Have you got any cheaper ones?
5. I'll take this skirt. Usually I don't wear skirts but this one is really nice.

[1] star [sta:] – *Star*

9 The Millennium Bridge (→ p. 30/ex. 2)

Read the text and put in the correct words.

had solved • had felt • had built
had decided • had chosen

After they had decided to build another bridge across the Thames, they started a competition. After they had chosen the architects, the work began in April 1999. After they had built the bridge, people started to walk across it. There were so many people on the bridge that it started to vibrate[1]. After a lot of people had felt sick on the bridge, they closed it. After they had solved the problem, they opened the bridge again in 2002. Now thousands of people use the Millennium Bridge every day.

10 A verb again (→ p. 30/ex. 2)

Work with a partner and find the past perfect forms for the rhymes. The fastest partner wins.

wake
buy
say
do ✔
know
see

1. For begin – had begun The rhyme is do – had done	4. For be – had been The rhyme is see – had seen
2. For catch – had caught The rhyme is buy – had bought	5. For fly – had flown The rhyme is know – had known
3. For speak – had spoken The rhyme is wake – had woken	6. For read – had read The rhyme is say – had said

11 On the bridge (→ p. 30/ex. 2)

Read what happened to Rüdiger, a German tourist. Complete the sentences. Think of your own ending for the last sentence.

hear a lot about it | read about the spectacular view | find it | forget to close my rucksack

1. I went to the Millennium Bridge because I had heard a lot about it.
2. I walked on the bridge because I had read about the spectacular view.
3. I lost my wallet because I had forgotten to close my rucksack.
4. A few minutes later, a girl gave it back to me because she had found it.
5. I was happy because I had a lot of money in it.

[1]to vibrate [vaɪˈbreɪt] – *virbrieren*

12 Life in the Tower (→ p. 30/ex. 2)

Look at the picture and complete the sentences. Use the simple past and the past perfect.

feed the chickens

pick flowers

make 20 cakes

wash the plates

clean the oven

In the 16th century Kate Warner worked in the Tower kitchen. One day, it was the Queen's birthday and Kate had a lot of work.

1. First she fed the chickens.
2. After she had fed the chickens, she picked the flowers.
3. After she had picked the flowers, she cleaned the oven.
4. After she had cleaned the oven, she made 20 cakes.
5. After she had made 20 cakes, she washed the plates.

13 Kate's story (→ p. 31/ex. 3)

Put in the correct verb forms: simple past or past perfect.

One day, someone escaped from the Tower prison. Kate was *(be)* scared. After she had fed *(feed)* the chickens, she stayed *(stay)* in the Tower kitchen. She didn't want *(not want)* to leave the kitchen. After the other girls had gone *(go)* to the Queen's dining room, Kate heard *(hear)* a strange noise. After she had looked *(look)* everywhere in the kitchen, she saw *(see)* a boy behind the cupboard. After she had seen *(see)* him, the boy came out *(come out)*. He said: "Yesterday I stole *(steal)* some bread. I was *(be)* hungry and my parents didn't have *(not have)* any money to buy food. After I had run *(run)* down the street, a policeman stopped *(stop)* me. He took *(take)* me to the Tower prison. But I escaped *(escape)*. Please, help me!" Kate was *(be)* very sorry and hid *(hide)* him in the kitchen. After everyone had gone *(go)* home in the evening, she helped *(help)* him to escape.

14 SKILLS: Skimming (→ p. 32/text)

a) *Before you read the text, answer the following questions with your partner.*

1. Look at the picture. What does it show?

It shows a boy with a black cat.

2. Read the title. What could the text be about?

A boy called Dick Whittington and his cat.

Dick Whittington and his cat

Most famous stories about London are about kings and queens. But do you know the story of a young boy and his cat? His name was Dick Whittington and he lived in the fourteenth century. Dick had no family, no home and no money. So he decided to go to London. When he arrived in the city, he was very tired, cold and hungry. But he was lucky because he met a man who gave him a job in his kitchen. Dick washed the dirty plates and carried wood for the fire. He had his own room, but he couldn't sleep at night because there were mice everywhere. One day, Dick found a small, black cat in a shopping bag. There were hundreds of mice in the house and the cat caught them.

The owner of the house was very happy about this. But Dick wasn't happy because the other men in the house didn't like his cat. So one night he left. He was very tired so he slept under a big tree. In the morning he heard some church bells. "Turn again, Whittington," they said. "Lord Mayor of London." So Dick went back to the man because he wanted to become Lord Mayor of London. One day, Dick opened the door of the living room. He had a lot of wood for the fire in his arms. His cat was with him. The cat caught a big mouse and brought it to Dick. A friend of the family was there, too. He had a lot of ships but there were always big mice on them. He needed a cat to catch them. So he borrowed Dick's cat for a few months. When the man brought back the cat, he gave Dick a lot of money because the cat had caught a lot of mice. Dick was now a rich man.

He became a businessman and married the man's daughter. Later he became Lord Mayor of London. But he never forgot his days as a young boy without a home and family. He used his money to build homes for children in London.

b) *Key words help you to understand the text. You can find the key words when you ask the questions: Who? What? When? Where? Why? Underline the key words with the right colour. Then fill in the grid.*

Who?	Dick Whittington, a small black cat, the owner of the house, a friend of the family, the man's daughter
What?	job, wash the dirty plates, carry wood for the fire, catch mice, a lot of ships, need a cat to catch mice, borrow Dick's cat, give Dick a lot of money, rich, businessman, marry, Lord Mayor of London
When?	fourteenth century one day, one night, in the morning, for a few months, later
Where?	London, in the kitchen, under a big tree, in the living room
Why?	no family, no home, no money, the other men in the house didn't like his cat, wanted to become Lord Mayor of London, there were always big mice, the cat had caught a lot of mice

15 Let's listen: Up and down (→ p. 33/ex. 1)

a) *Listen to the CD. Now read the sentences. Where do the voices go up? Where do they go down? Draw ↓ or ↑ in the boxes.*

1. This is a really fantastic city [↓]. There's so much to see and do [↓].
2. Tomorrow it will be sunny in the morning [↑] and wet in the afternoon [↓].
3. Please bring us a pizza [↑], the spaghetti [↑] and a lemonade [↓].
4. I know you like old ships [↑], so let's visit the Cutty Sark [↓].
5. After we've been to the Tower [↑], we can come back to Westminster by boat [↓].

b) *Listen again and check your answers. Work with a partner and try to say the sentences in a) correctly. The signs in the boxes will help you.*

16 Let's listen: Could I have your attention, please? (→ p. 33/ex. 3)

Which picture in each pair gives the information in the announcement: A or B?

17 Let's listen: Opinions about London (→ p. 33/ex. 3)

Listen and find out what the visitor thinks about London. Put a x *in the correct box.*

	right	wrong	not in the dialogue
1. Some museums are boring.		x	
2. Everything is expensive.	x		
3. British people never wait in queues.		x	
4. The streets are dirty.			x
5. The food is terrible.		x	
6. There aren't enough parks.		x	
7. Life is faster in Britain.	x		
8. People are polite.	x		

18 Information, please! (→ p. 33/ex. 3)

You are in London with your friend. Each of you knows something which the other one wants to know. Ask each other questions and let your partner give the answers. You can find the information in the pictures.

A

- frage, wie du zum Tower kommst

(Take the Circle Line to Tower Hill.
Excuse me, where are the nearest toilets?)

WC | ***St. James's Park***

- frage, wieviel ein Ticket nach Tower Hill kostet

(A ticket to Tower Hill is 3 pounds.
Is there a post office near here?)

Covent Garden

- frage, wieviel eine Postkarte nach Deutschland kostet

(A postcard to Germany is 44 pence.
When is the zoo open today?)

- frage, welches das größte Geschäft in London ist

(Harrods is the biggest shop in London.
What is the scariest museum?)

B

(Excuse me, how do I get to the Tower?)

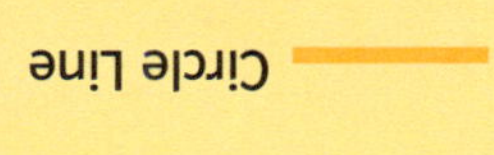

- frage, wo die nächsten Toiletten sind

(The nearest toilets are in St. James's Park.
How much is a ticket to Tower Hill?)

- frage, ob es in der Nähe eine Post gibt

(There is a post office at Covent Garden.
How much is a postcard to Germany?)

- frage, wann der Zoo heute geöffnet hat

(The zoo is open from 10:00 to 17:30 today.
What is the biggest shop in London?)

- frage, welches das gruseligste Museum ist

(The London Dungeons is the scariest museum.)

19 Describe a person (→ p. 35/ex. 3)

a) *Read the text about Pru again. Underline all the key words in the text.*

"Hi, I'm Pru! No, I'm not a punk! I'm a hairdresser at Accent in Shoreditch – I only began there last year but I've already learnt to do some fantastic styles – and I learn more every day. I really love my work there. It is more like a hobby to me. When I left school, I worked in a post office but it was a bit boring. This job is different. You know, a few of my regulars are big names on TV and they chat to me about their lives. I can tell you, it's as exciting as any of those TV soaps! I once got so interested in a spicy story that I made a real mess of the woman's hair. But I was lucky – she just thought it was a cool, new style!"

b) *Look at the photo and describe Pru. The following questions can help you.*

1. What can you say about her age? Is she young or old? She is young.
2. Look at her clothes. Do you think she likes fashion? She likes fashion.
3. What about her hairstyle? She has got a cool hairstyle.

c) *Use your key words and the information from the photo to make a mind map about Pru.*

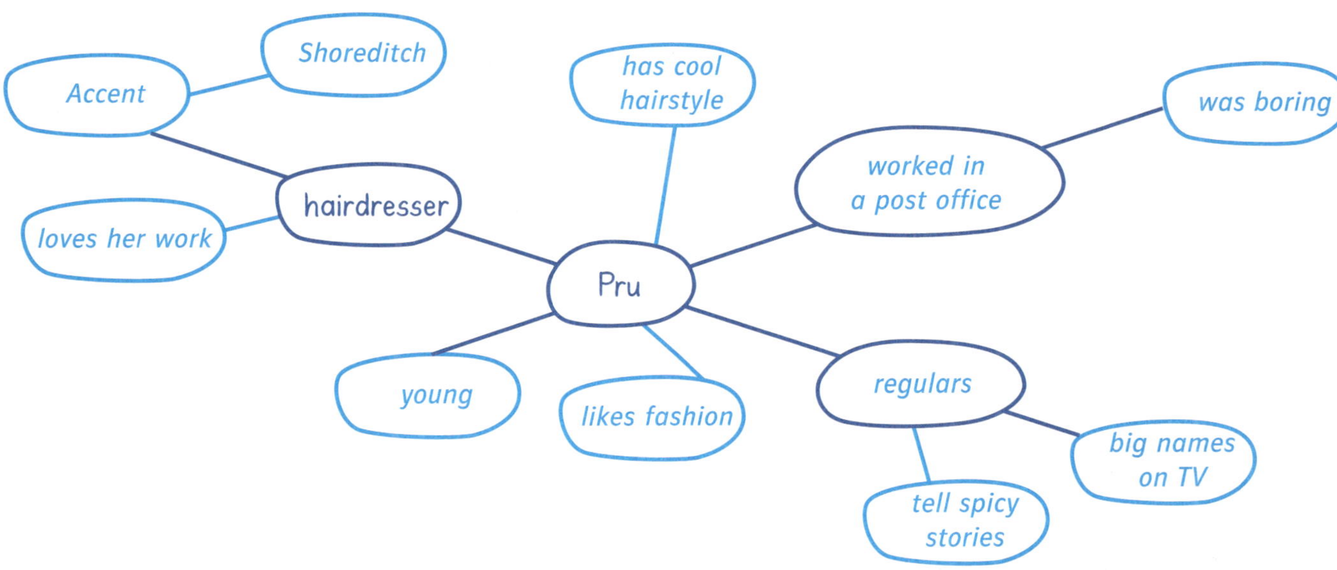

d) *Use the information from the mind map and write a short text about Pru. You can start like this:*

Pru is a hairdresser at Accent in Shoreditch. She is young, likes fashion and has a cool hairstyle. Pru loves her work. She worked in a post office but that was boring. A few of Pru's regulars are big names on TV. They tell her spicy stories.

20 A London puzzle (→ p. 36/ex. 1)

Find the missing words and fill the crossword puzzle.

1. Some people really have a strange … ! They wear funny clothes.
2. He … to help me with my homework.
3. You need … to make a fire.
4. My room is always a … !
5. A long time ago people built houses with wood and … .
6. The fire … for four hours.
7. Oh no! My brother has read my … .
8. May I have a … of cake, please?
9. The storm … a lot of houses last night.
10. "I don't want to … about the new CD with you!"
11. "I could … the pizza before I walked in the kitchen."
12. They can open … for ships.

				12↓						
1→			S	T	Y	L	E			
2→				O	F	F	E	R	E	D
3→				W	O	O	D			
4→			M	E	S	S				
5→		S	T	R	A	W				
6→				B	U	R	N	T		
7→	D	I	A	R	Y					
8→			P	I	E	C	E			
9→				D	A	M	A	G	E	D
10→		A	R	G	U	E				
11→		S	M	E	L	L				

21 Word pairs (→ p. 36/ex.2)

Which words in the box go with the pairs of words?

building | clothes | museum | jewel | person | newspaper | pollution | smoke | view

1. beautiful, valuable – *jewel*
2. expensive, trendy – *clothes*
3. clear, spectacular – *view*
4. rich, sporty – *person*
5. evening, national – *newspaper*
6. thick, black – *smoke*
7. huge, stone – *building*
8. interesting, art – *museum*
9. air, terrible – *pollution*

22 Silly sentences (→ p. 37/ex. 6)

Just one or two different letters can make a very different word! Underline the wrong words in these sentences, and then write down the correct word.

1. Let's find a nice palace where we can sit down and eat our sandwiches. – *place*
2. Wow! That big crowd must be a terrible weight on the Queen's head! – *crown*
3. Our bus isn't moving in this traffic ham, so let's get off and walk. – *jam*
4. Hey, you mustn't take my picture with my hair in a message like this! – *mess*
5. That courier over there must know the streets like the back of her head. – *hand*
6. This model of Robbie Williams looks just like the royal Robbie! – *real*

23 A quick word game (→ p. 37/ex. 6)

Work with a partner. Write down: BUCKINGHAM PALACE. How many English words can you make with these letters in three minutes? Who's fastest? (individuelle Schülerlösung)

24 Complete the dialogue with simple past forms (→ p. 38/ex. 2)

be | have | help | start | decide | not like

A: When *did* ______ you *start* ______ your job at the London Dungeon?

B: Last month. Before that I *had* ______ a job in an office.

A: Why *did* ______ you *decide* ______ to change jobs?

B: Because I *didn't like* ______ my old boss. She *was* ______ a scary woman.

A: Scary? Oh well, that *helped* ______ you for your new job here!

25 Put in: *one – ones* (→ p. 39/ex. 3)

I like zoos, and last weekend I went to the *one* ______ in London. It's a really good *one* ______ with lots of different animals. The lions were very interesting. There was a big *one* ______ and two smaller *ones* ______. They weren't scary because they slept. Then I went to the tigers. There was an old *one* ______ who looked a bit sad. Then the tigers got some food and they were all happy. My favourite animals were the elephants. There was a funny *one* ______ who waved his ears at me. And there were also two young *ones* ______. They were really sweet.

26 Put in past perfect forms (→ p. 39/ex. 4)

Yesterday morning Lucy asked her mum for some money to go to the hairdresser. After her mum *had given* ______ *(give)* her the money, she left the house. She was happy and very excited. A week ago she *had decided* ______ *(decide)* to become a punk. But, of course, she *hadn't told* ______ *(not tell)* her mother. After she *had arrived* ______ *(arrive)* at the hairdresser, she was even more excited. She sat down and read some magazines. After she *had waited* ______ *(wait)* for half an hour, she told the hairdresser about her plan to become a punk. The hairdresser started his work. He *had done* ______ *(do)* it before. He made her hair short and green. After he *had finished* ______ *(finish)*, Lucy looked at the mirror[1]. There was a strange noise. She opened her eyes. Her alarm clock *had just made* ______ *(just make)* the noise – it was only a dream.

[1] mirror ['mɪrə] – *Spiegel*

1 Write the story (→ p. 40/ex. 2)

a) *Look at the pictures and put in the missing words.*

1. Yesterday morning Leo's owner left the house. 2. Leo was hungry and went to the fish bowl. 3. Then Leo jumped on the table and tried to catch Goldy. Goldy was scared. 4. Suddenly, another fish came out from behind a plant. It caught Leo's tail[1]. 5. That hurt a lot and Leo dropped Goldy and jumped off the table. 6. Goldy was very happy because her boyfriend had saved her.

b) *Think of a title for the story.* A dangerous cat

2 Make one sentence from two with conjunctions (→ p. 40/ex. 3)

and | because | but | when | which

1. Leo's owner was not at home. Leo was hungry.
   Leo's owner was not at home and Leo was hungry.
2. Leo jumped on the table. Leo wanted to catch Goldy.
   Leo jumped on the table because he wanted to catch Goldy.
3. Leo had Goldy. Another fish came from behind a plant.
   Leo had Goldy when another fish came from behind a plant.

3 Make the sentences more interesting (→ p. 40/ex. 3)

Look at the pictures again and add your own adjectives and adverbs.

1. Leo was very hungry. 2. He hungrily jumped on the table. 3. Another fish hid angrily behind a plant. 4. Leo shouted loudly. 5. Goldy looked happily at her boyfriend. 6. Leo's tail hurt badly.

[1] tail [teɪl] – *Schwanz*

Unit 3 Here we come!

1 A quiz (→ p. 45/ex. 2)

Do you know the answers to this quiz?

I'm very old. You can find me near Salisbury.

Stonehenge

We are very famous. You can see us from the ferry.

White Cliffs of Dover

I'm an important port of the South of England.

Southampton

People love my beaches.

Brighton

I'm the largest airport in the UK.

Heathrow

People who don't want to fly use me to come to the UK.

Channel Tunnel

2 A city in the south (→ p. 45/ex. 3)

a) *Read the article about Southampton. Underline everything which you can see or visit there.*

Sea city Southampton

Southampton is the number one port for cruise ships in the UK. There you can see one of the famous cruise ships like the Queen Elizabeth 2. You can even take a short cruise yourself (on a much smaller boat, of course) and get a better view of these huge, fantastic ships. Southampton is also the greenest city in south England. It has many beautiful parks and gardens. The huge Mayfield Park, west of the city, is a popular place to go. But make sure the wild ponies don't eat your sandwiches! Of course you can also have a nice cup of English tea and a sandwich at one of the many cafés in Oxford Street. After that you can go shopping in almost a hundred different shops. Southampton has something for everyone!

b) *Put circles around three places in the text which you find most interesting. Tell your partner about them.* *(individuelle Schülerlösung)*

c) *There are two other famous cruise ships wich you can see in Southampton. Find out their names on the Internet.*

1. *Queen Mary 2*

2. *Freedom of the Seas*

3 I can ..., but I can't .... (→ p. 46/ex. 2)

a) *Read the three rhymes. Can you guess what the different things are?*

1. I can move on the sea,
   but I can't climb a tree.
   When I see sand,
   I know I'm near land

   wave

2. I can make you angry,
   but you can't catch me.
   I'm a kind of jam,
   tell me what I am!

   traffic jam

3. You can press me,
   but you can't pull me.
   I'm near to the door,
   but I'm not on the floor.

   button

b) *Can you make up a rhyme? Write it in your exercise book. Start with 'I can ..., but I can't ...'. Read it to your partner and let him or her guess the answer.* (individuelle Schülerlösung)

4 Let's get ready for the beach! (→ p. 46/ex. 2)

You are getting ready for the beach. Look at the pictures and say what you must bring and what you needn't bring to the beach.

Must	Needn't
I must bring my swimsuit.	I needn't bring my boots.
I must bring my sandwiches.	I needn't bring my coat.
I must bring a blanket.	I needn't bring a map.
I must bring my shorts.	
I must bring two bottles of water.	

5 Birdy on the beach (→ p. 46/ex. 2)

Birdy lives on the beach in Brighton. He likes to play with the tourists. His mum has given him a note with rules. Look at the rules and write down what Birdy must or mustn't do.

1. He mustn't sit on people's heads.
2. He must fly around regulary.
3. He mustn't eat the people's sandwiches.
4. He must look for food in the rubbish.
5. He mustn't come home too late.
6. He mustn't bully the other birds.
7. He must be nice to the lifeguard.

Please,
- don't sit on people's heads
- fly around regularly
- don't eat the people's sandwiches
- look for food in the rubbish
- don't come home too late
- don't bully the other birds
- be nice to the lifeguard

6 Birdy's questions (→ p. 47/ex. 3)

Birdy has found some fish and chips and a big piece of chocolate cake in the rubbish. He has brought the food home. What does he ask his mum?

leave some fish for my sister • eat fish and chips first • go out after dinner • look for tomorrow's dinner, too • wash my feet before dinner • have some cake

1. Can I have some cake? — Yes, you can. But only for dessert.
2. *Must I eat fish and chips first?* — Yes, you must. Fish is very healthy.
3. *Must I leave some fish for my sister?* — No, you needn't. Your sister doesn't like fish.
4. *Must I wash my feet before dinner?* — Yes, you must. Dirty feet are terrible.
5. *Can I go out after dinner?* — Yes, you can. But you must be back before it gets dark.
6. *Can I look for tomorrow's dinner, too?* — No, you needn't. Your dad will catch some fish tomorrow.

7 What's Fred thinking? (→ p. 47/ex. 3)

Fred wants to go swimming. Find out what he is thinking. Put in 'must' or 'needn't'.

1. I *must* listen to the lifeguard, but I *needn't* worry.
2. I *must* take some money with me to buy an ice-cream, but I *needn't* take more than £20.
3. It's very hot, so I *must* wear a T-shirt, but I *needn't* wear shorts.
4. I *needn't* swim with my rubber ring, but I *must* be careful because I can't swim a long way alone.

8 What about your country? (→ p. 47/ex. 4)

Fred lives in England. He wants to spend the holidays in Germany, but he has never been there before. Write him a short e-mail and tell him what he can, can't, must, mustn't and needn't do in your country. The words in the box can help you, but use some of your own ideas, too. Write in your exercise book. *(individuelle Schülerlösung)*

drive left/right

sauerkraut

pound/euro

9 Photos from England (→ p. 48/ex. 1)

Look at these photos. What can you see? Complete the sentences and use 'who' or 'which'.

1. That's an English milkman who delivers milk to the houses in the morning.
2. These are signs which have Irish names on them.
3. This is an information board which shows the different flights at the airport.
4. These are the famous cliffs which are near Dover.
5. That's a plane which is landing at Heathrow Airport.
6. That's the clock Big Ben which signals the New Year at midnight on 31st December.

10 A trip to the south of England (→ p. 48/ex. 2)

a) *Read this article from a travel magazine. Correct the text and make it more interesting. Always put two sentences together and use 'who' or 'whose'.*

A trip to the south of England

Peter Show from London was our guide. ~~He~~ who showed us a lot of interesting places.

First he took us to Brighton. ~~Its~~ whose beach was great.

In the bus I met a tourist from Italy. ~~He~~ who was in England for the first time.

Then we went to Stonehenge. ~~Its~~ whose ancient circle of stones was a bit scary.

In Southampton I talked to a woman in Mayfield Park. ~~She~~ who was once on the Queen Elizabeth 2.

Our last stop was Dover. ~~The~~ whose White Cliffs looked very beautiful.

b) *Write the new text in your exercise book.*

11 What's this? (→ p. 49/text) (individuelle Schülerlösung)

Look at these pictures. Write one sentence for each picture in your exercise book. Use relative clauses with 'that'. Read the sentences to your partner. Can he/she find the correct picture?
Example: A postcard is something that you send your friends when you are on holiday.

12 A dark day in history (→ p. 49/ex. 3)

Decide if the phrases of time are in the correct place and put a ✗ in the correct box.

1. a) The Titanic was ready to make its first trip on 10th April 1912. [ ]
   b) On 10th April 1912 the Titanic was ready to make its first trip. [ ]
   c) Both sentences are correct. [x]

2. a) For the first few days everyone had fun on the huge ocean liner. [x]
   b) Everyone had fun for the first few days on the ocean liner. [ ]
   c) Both sentences are correct. [ ]

3. a) The passengers every evening enjoyed good food and parties. [ ]
   b) The passengers enjoyed good food and parties every evening. [x]
   c) Both sentences are correct. [ ]

4. a) The Titanic hit ice at around 23:40 the next day. [ ]
   b) At around 23:40 the next day the Titanic hit ice. [ ]
   c) Both sentences are correct. [x]

5. a) One hour later most of the passengers tried to get into a few small boats. [x]
   b) Most of the passengers one hour later tried to get into a few small boats. [ ]
   c) Both sentences are correct. [ ]

6. a) At 2:20 the Titanic and 1,522 people on the ship went under water. [ ]
   b) The Titanic and 1,522 people on the ship went under water at 2.20. [ ]
   c) Both sentences are correct. [x]

13 Elizabeth's story (→ p. 49/ex. 4)

Elizabeth was one of the women who travelled on the Titanic with a friend. Look at the pictures and write her story. Use the phrases of place and time in the box.

one our later • at 23:40 • at 22:00 • on Sunday evening ✔ • at 2:20 • in the early hours of the morning • into the water • into a boat • in our beds • in the ship's restaurant ✔ • into a boat • to bed

1. On Sunday evening we had dinner in the ship's restaurant.

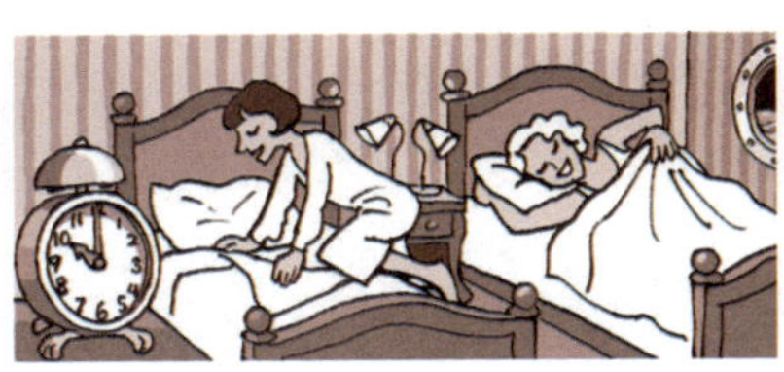

2. At 22:00 we went to bed.

3. At 23:40 we woke up in our beds.

4. One hour later we tried to get into a boat.

5. At 2:20 we jumped into the water.

6. In the early hours of the morning we climbed into a boat.

14 SKILLS: Be polite (→ p. 50/ex. 1)

Look at these dialogues and complete them.

1. A: I'm sorry to bother you, but could you please put your bag in the locker?
   B: *Yes, of course.*
2. A: *Excuse me, what happens when we arrive at the airport?*
   B: You must go through Passports and Customs.
3. A: Could you help me please? I can't find my seat.
   B: *Yes, of course. Your seat is over there.*
4. A: *Would you like something to eat?*
   B: I'd like a sandwich, please.
5. A: Excuse me. Could you please give me a blanket? I'm cold.
   B: *Yes, of course. Here you are.*

15 Bob needs help (→ p. 50/ex. 2)

a) *Bob is travelling to London but he needs some help on the way. What can he ask the people?*

Excuse me, where are the trolleys?

Excuse me, I can't find the information desk.

I'd like a sandwich, please.

Excuse me, can you tell me the gate number?

b) *Act dialogues with your partner. Use the questions from a). Your partner thinks of the answers.*

c) *Think of two other situations. Write dialogues in your exercise book.* *(individuelle Schülerlösung)*

16 Let's listen: Your passport, please! (→ p. 51/ex. 1)

Read the sentences and decide if they are right or wrong. Put a ✗ in the correct boxes.

	Right	Wrong
1. Jens needs a new passport.	✗	
2. Jens didn't pack the bags himself.		✗
3. Some kids gave Jens some chocolate cake.		✗
4. The officer asked Jens to show him his laptop.	✗	
5. The officer was very angry.		✗
6. Jens and Steffi missed their train.		✗

17 At the train station (→ p. 51/ex. 2)

These people at the train station aren't very friendly.
Can you make their questions and answers more polite?

How much is it to Bristol? — £8.

1. "Excuse me, could you tell me how much it is to Bristol, please?" "Of course, it's £8."

I want to buy a map. — £3.75.

2. "I'd like a map, please."
"That's £ 3.75, please."

Give me a cup of tea. — With sugar?

3. "I'd like a cup of tea, please."
"Would you like sugar?"

Where are the toilets? — Over there.

4. "Excuse me, where are the toilets?"
"The toilets are over there."

You've dropped your wallet. — Oh.

5. "Excuse me, you've dropped your wallet."
"Oh, thank you!"

18 Let's listen: Where's Susi? (→ p. 51/ex. 2)

Listen to Kevin and his Mum at a department store in Brighton and answer the questions.

1. What does Kevin want to do? He wants to go to the beach.
2. What has happened to Susi? They have lost her.
3. Who do Kevin and his mum ask for help? They ask the assistant for help.
4. Describe Susi. She's 5, has brown hair and is wearing a red T-shirt.
5. Where can Kevin and his mum find Susi? They can find her at the information desk.

19 Mediation and communication: Signs (→ p. 51/ex. 3)

Look at these signs from the British Isles. Tell your partner where the different signs are from. The word boxes can help you.

in Welsh 'hir' means 'long'

'loch' is the word for 'lake' in Scotland.

Great Blasket Island is near the west coast of Ireland

the Cornish word for 'Falmouth' is 'Aberfal'

A

(Das Schild ist aus Cornwall, weil das kornische Wort ‚Aberfal' ‚Falmouth' bedeutet.)

(Das Schild ist aus Schottland, weil ‚loch' in Schottland ‚See' bedeutet.)

B

(Das Schild ist aus Irland, weil Great Blasket Island an der irischenWestküste liegt.)

(Das Schild ist aus Wales, weil ‚hir' auf Walisisch ‚lang' bedeutet.)

20 Mediation and communication: At the train station (→ p. 51/ex. 3)

You are at the train station in Brighton. There is a German boy who doesn't speak English very well. He asks you to go to the information desk with him. Work with a partner and complete the dialogues. You fill in the yellow parts and your partner fills in the blue parts.

Boy: Frage bitte, wann der nächste Zug nach London fährt.

You: When does the next train *to London leave?*

Assistant[1]: The next train to London leaves at 14:30.

You: *Der nächste Zug nach London fährt um 14:30.*

Boy: Frage bitte, an welchem Bahnsteig der Zug abfährt.

You: *From which platform does the train leave?*

Assistant: The train leaves from platform 3.

You: *Der Zug fährt vom Bahnsteig 3 ab.*

[1] assistant [əˈsɪstnt] – *hier: Bahnangestellte/r*

21 SKILLS: A summary (→ p. 53/ex. 4)

a) *Read this text about a famous smuggler and underline all the key words in the text.*

A real smuggler

Lots of famous heroes in books or films are smugglers with exciting but terrible adventures. But were any of them real men? And were their adventures really as fantastic as in these stories? If you travel along the south coast of England, you will see lots of clues that point to smugglers. One example is a farm near Bournemouth[1] which belonged to Isaac Gulliver[2], a famous local smuggler hero. He was born on 5th September 1745. Later he lived near the south coast in 'Gulliver's House'.

Many people think that smugglers are horrible people who customs officials try to catch. But they often escape and get out of trouble. There is one thing that makes Isaac Gulliver different from other smugglers: People who have written about him all say that he was a very friendly person. He used his head and found it easy to guess other people's plans. They also say he never killed a man in his long life as a smuggler. So he wasn't just lucky to become one of the richest men in the area! As he built up smuggler activities, he also built up a 'normal life'. He married a nice girl and took over her father's inn[3] so the people thought that was his normal job. But this inn was very near the coast where he picked up his goods[4]. It was also not far from a place which other smugglers used for the 'exchange' of their goods.

Gulliver smuggled[5] lots of things like tea, wine[6] and whisky[7]. As he made money, he didn't just spend it quickly. Instead of this he bought more land, another inn and a few farms near the coast so it was easier for him to smuggle and hide his goods. They say he even hid some goods in a church! The customs officers knew about his activities but they just couldn't catch the greatest and nicest smuggler of the time.

Gulliver died in 1822 and you can visit the church where he lies.

b) *Use your key words and write a summary of the text. Remember to keep your text short and to use the simple present. You can start like this:*

The text "A real smuggler" is about Isaac Gulliver. He *was a famous local smuggler hero.*

He was born on 5th September 1745. Isaac Gulliver was different from other smugglers. He was a very friendly person. He never killed a man in his long life. Gulliver built up a normal life, married a girl and took over an inn. This inn was near the coast and he could smuggle tea, wine and whisky. Gulliver became very rich and the customs officers couldn't catch him. He died in 1822.

[1] Bournemouth ['bɔ:nməθ] – *Stadt in Südengland,* [2] Isaac Gulliver [ˌaɪzək 'gʌlɪvə], [3] inn [ɪn] – *Wirtshaus,* [4] goods [gʊdz] – *Waren,* [5] to smuggle ['smʌgl] – *schmuggeln,* [6] wine [waɪn] – *Wein,* [7] whisky ['wɪski] – *Whisky*

22 At the airport (→ p. 54/ex. 1)

Make a mind map.

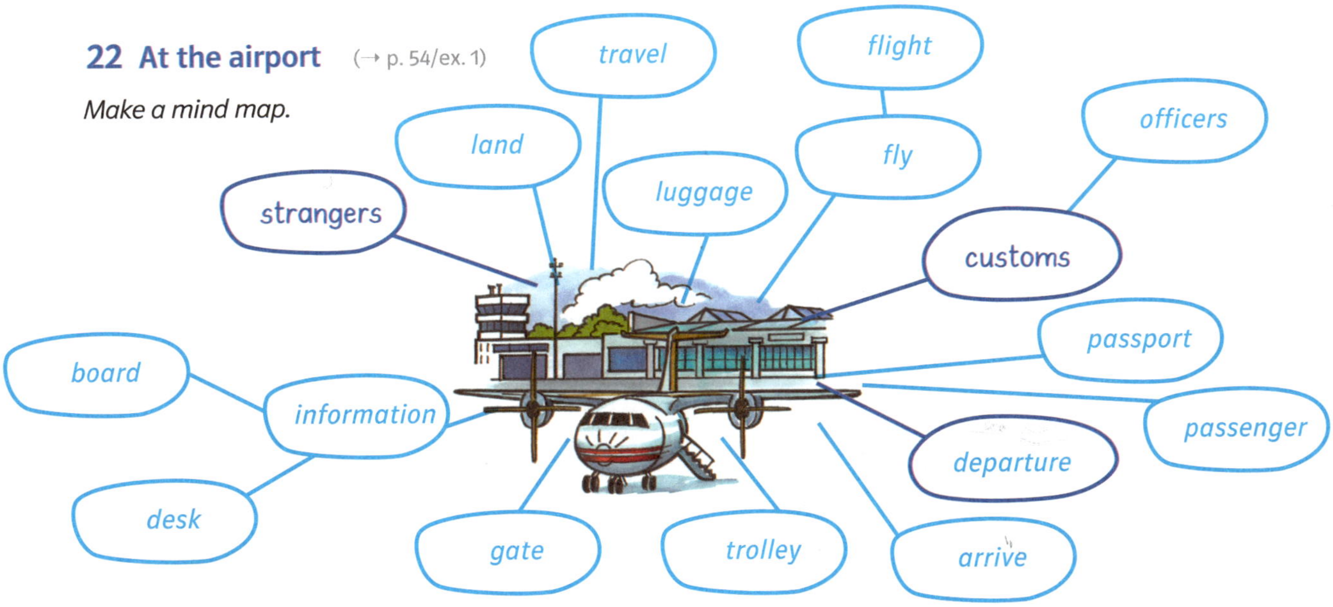

23 What are all these people saying? (→ p. 54/ex. 3)

Find the correct parts of the sentences and find out what the different people are saying.

1. You must be sensible now,	it was like paradise.
2. I don't know how I lost my passport,	he was furious with me.
3. I hope you locked the	so I've got my own flat.
4. I dropped my father's aftershave and	you can't go diving just after lunch.
5. I need to find my mobile	and came out into this huge cave.
6. You can't imagine the place,	door when you left?
7. We crawled through this small tunnel	it's a real mystery to me.
8. I am a very independent person,	so I can ring my parents.

24 Fantastic weights and measurements! (→ p. 55/ex. 4)

a) *Read the texts about Sandy and Jon. Put the weights and measurements into kilos and metres.*

The heaviest man

The heaviest man in history was Jon Brower Minnoch from the USA. He was 6ft 1" (1.86m) tall and had a weight of 28st (177 kg) in 1963. Jon just got bigger and bigger. In 1966 he was 50st (317 kg), in 1976 he was 69st 9lbs (442 kg) and by the time he went to hospital in 1978, the doctors said he was over 100st (635 kg). After almost two years in hospital, he was down to 34st (215 kg) and the doctors let him go home. It was very sad that three years later, he was again 68st (431 kg). On 10th September 1983 Jon died. He was 57st (361 kg).

The tallest woman

When Sandy Allen came into the world in June 1955, she was a normal baby at 6.5lbs (2.25 kg). But soon after this she became taller and taller. By the time she was 10 years old, she was 6ft 3" (189.9 m) tall. At the age of 16, she had reached the height of 7ft 1" (215.8 m). Life can't be much fun when you are so tall, but Sandy was lucky to find a boyfriend who was at least almost as tall as her. He was 7ft (213.4 m).

b) *Imagine you are Jon or Sally. How do you feel? Talk about it with a partner.* (individuelle Schülerlösung)

[1]Jon Brower Minnoch [dʒɒn ˌbraʊə ˈmɪnək], [2]Sandy Allen [sændi ˈæln]

25 What can they do? (→ p. 56/ex. 3)

Complete these senteces.

1. Your shoes are dirty. You *mustn't* walk into the house with them.
2. I have already read all these books. You *can* have them now.
3. I'm sorry, I *can't* tell you the way to the post office. I don't know where it is.
4. Oh, the dog is really hungry. I *must* feed him now.
5. I've already bought everything we need. You *needn't* go to the supermarket.

can | can't | must | mustn't | needn't

26 The courier (→ p. 57/ex. 4)

Do you remember the story 'The courier'? Put in 'who' or 'which'.

1. Sue was a girl *who* was blind.
2. There were two men *who* were smugglers.
3. It was the smugglers *who* followed Sue and her parents home.
4. It was their car *which* stopped on the other side of the street.
5. The two men found Sue *who* lived in the basement of her parents house.
6. Sue smelt the same aftershave *which* she had smelt at Moscow and Heathrow Airports.
7. Sue found the fuse-box *which* was on the wall.
8. It was a neighbour *who* heard Sue and came to help her.

27 Phrases of time and place (→ p. 57/ex. 6) *(Lösungsvorschlag)*

Use a word or phrase from each box and write holiday sentences.

Place	Verb	Time
Brighton ✔ • hotel • restaurant • France • queue • Southampton	wait • windsurf • go • stay • fly • meet	Last night • two hours • last summer • every year ✔ • around 1 pm • for two weeks

We go to Brighton on holiday every year.

Last night we went to a restaurant in Southampton.

We flew to France last summer.

We waited in a queue for two hours.

We went windsurfing in France last summer.

We stayed at a hotel for two weeks.

1 A good advert? (→ p. 59/ex. 1)

Look at this advert and answer the questions. (Lösungsvorschlag)

1. What is this advert for?
   It's an advert for Stonehenge.
2. What can you say about the picture?
   It shows Stonehenge. It's foggy and very pink.
3. What does the advert want you to do?
   It wants you to go to Stonehenge.
4. What do you think about the text? The text is good. It says that there is a mystery at Stonehenge.
5. Is this an advert which you will remember? Why or why not?
   Yes, because I like the colours and the text.

2 An advert for ice-cream (→ p. 59/ex. 3)

a) *Make an advert for ice-cream. Look at the pictures. What do you think about them?*

1 

This picture is nice. The ice-cream looks good.

2 

This picture doesn't show ice-cream.

3 

You can't see the ice-cream very well.

b) *Choose one of the pictures for your advert.* Picture 1

c) *You also need a short text for your advert. Look at the different texts. What can you say about them?*

... BECAUSE IT TASTES GREAT!	Eat me!	CAN YOU THINK OF ANYTHING BETTER?
This text is OK. It's a bit long.	This text is good. It's short.	This text is too long.

d) *Choose one of the texts for your advert.* 2

e) *Show your picture and text to your partner. What does he/she think about it?* (individuelle Schülerlösung)

Meine Lernbiografie 2

Jetzt hast du die ersten drei Units bearbeitet. Male zu jedem Satz einen Smiley in der entsprechenden Farbe. An welchen Stellen hast du „muss ich noch üben" ausgewählt? Nimm dir diese Bereiche in den nächsten Wochen noch einmal genau vor. Frage auch deinen Lehrer/deine Lehrerin, ob er/sie dir Tipps geben kann.

Was ich alles kann!

sehr gut   gut   muss ich noch üben

			Übung im ... Seite/Übung
Hören	Ich kann Hörtexten einzelne Informationen entnehmen und Fragen zum Gehörten beantworten.		Schülerbuch S. 26/2, 33/1, 45/3 Workbook S. 23/16, 17, S. 35/16, 18
	Ich verstehe auch längere Hörtexte und kann Teile daraus wiedergeben.		Schülerbuch S. 33/3, S. 51/1, 2
Sprechen	Ich kann eine Wegbeschreibung geben.		Schülerbuch S. 37/4 Workbook S. 24
	Ich kann ein Foto beschreiben.		Schülerbuch S. 27/3 Workbook S. 17/1
	Ich kann über Ereignisse in der Vergangenheit berichten.		Schülerbuch S. 28/1 Workbook S. 18/3, 4, 5, S. 19/6, 7
	Ich kann Handlungen und Ereignisse in der Vergangenheit mit ‚*after*' und ‚*when*' beschreiben.		Schülerbuch S. 30/2, S. 31/3, 4 Workbook S. 7/12, 13
	Ich kann die Modalverben richtig anwenden.		Schülerbuch S. 47/4 Workbook S. 30/4, 5, S. 31/6, 7, 8
	Ich kann Relativsätze bilden.		Schülerbuch S. 48/1, 2 Workbook S. 32/9, 10, 11
	Ich kann Orts- und Zeitangaben an die richtige Stelle im Satz setzen.		Schülerbuch S. 49/3, 4 Workbook S. 33/12, 13
	Ich kann mich höflich ausdrücken.		Schülerbuch S. 50/1, 2, 3 Workbook S. 34/14, 15, S. 35/17
	Ich kann einen englischen Dialog/englische Hinweisschilder auf Deutsch wiedergeben.		Workbook S. 36/19, 20
Lesen	Ich kann längere Geschichten lesen und verstehen.		Schülerbuch S. 53/2
	Ich kann Einzelheiten aus Texten herausfinden und Aufgaben dazu lösen.		Schülerbuch S. 35/2 Workbook S. 29/2
	Ich kann die wichtigsten Punkte aus einem Text entnehmen (Skimming).		Schülerbuch S. 32 Workbook S. 22/14

Schreiben	Ich kann einen Ort, ein Gebäude oder eine Person beschreiben.		Schülerbuch S. 31/4 Workbook S. 25/19
	Ich kann ein Foto beschreiben.		Schülerbuch S. 35/5
	Ich kann einen Tagebucheintrag schreiben.		Schülerbuch S. 35/3
	Ich kann eine Bildergeschichte schreiben.		Schülerbuch S. 40–41 Workbook S. 28
	Ich kann ein *summary* schreiben.		Schülerbuch S. 53/4 Workbook S. 37/21
	Ich kann eine Werbeanzeige gestalten.		Schülerbuch S. 59/3 Workbook S. 40/2

Was ich noch besser machen kann!

Schreibe wieder auf, welche Erfahrungen du beim Lernen gemacht hast und woran du in nächster Zeit arbeiten willst.

Konntest du die Ziele, die du dir nach Unit 1 gesetzt hast, erreichen? Was konntest du verbessern?

____

____

Welche Schwierigkeiten tauchten beim Lernen auf? Wie konntest du sie überwinden?

____

____

Worauf bist du in dieser Lerneinheit besonders stolz?

____

Was möchtest du in Zukunft noch stärker üben?

____

____

Tipps von deinem Lehrer/deiner Lehrerin:

____

____

Datum: ______________ Unterschrift: ______________________________

Unit 4 Let it out!

1 Problems, problems (→ p. 52/ex. 1) (Lösungsvorschlag)

These parents and teenagers are having problems with each other. What are they saying? Write dialogues for the pictures.

1. Mum: "Clean your room! It looks terrible."
   Girl: "No! It's my room! Leave me alone!"

2. Mum: "You don't work hard enough for school!"
   Boy: "But I do my homework every day!"

3. Dad: "Those people are horrible!"
   Boy: "But they are my friends!"

4. Dad: "You can't go out after dinner!"
   Girl: "But I want to go out with my friends!"

2 Video slams (→ p. 52/ex. 3)

a) *Read this information about a video slam and answer the questions.*

VIDEO SLAM!

- THE SLAM IS OPEN TO EVERYONE
- MAKE YOUR OWN FILM ABOUT A SUBJECT WHICH YOU FIND INTERESTING
- YOU SHOW YOUR FILM TO THE AUDIENCE AND TO THE JUDGES
- THE JUDGES GIVE YOU POINTS FOR YOUR FILM
- THE BEST FILM WINS £500

ENTER NOW AND SHOW YOUR FILM AT THE SLAM!

1. Who can take part in a video slam? Everyone can take part.
2. What do you show at a video slam? You show your own film.
3. What does the winner get? The winner gets £ 500.

b) *Would you like to take part in a poetry slam or in a video slam? Why/Why not?* (individuelle Schülerlösung)

3 Where is it? (→ p. 54/ex. 1)

There is one sentence in the puzzle. Can you find it? Write the sentence.

WRTZHBSDHNKMLAURENWQCVBZPLKHWILLBFWLPSDVCTHNNKPFGMKMOVESDF
GHJJJTOHGWRTZBFVGHKLPZHNBTCORNWALLWDFGHBVNCQWSOONKRGBDXJZHL

Lauren will move to Cornwall soon.

4 Lauren's poem (→ p. 54/ex. 2)

Lauren is sad. She has written a poem in her diary. Put in the correct words.

I'm sure the village *will be* very small
and the new garden *will mean* work for us all.
I *'ll have to get up* early to get to school
and my new teachers *will be* awful, not cool.
I *'ll miss* my friends when I'm away
and I *'ll be* very sad on my birthday in May.
My little cat Buffy *will be* my only friend
but I hope I *'ll find* some more friends in the end.

'll find | 'll be | 'll have to get up | 'll miss | 'll feel | will be | will mean

5 Will I need this? (→ p. 54/ex. 3)

Lauren is packing her things. She is thinking about the things she will or won't keep. Complete the sentences.

1. Maybe I *'ll throw away* (*throw away*) this poster because I probably *won't hang up* (*not hang up*) this old poster again.
2. I think I *won't take* (*not take*) this skirt with me because it is too small, but maybe Nyla *will want* (*want*) it.
3. I think I *'ll leave* (*leave*) the old wardrobe here because there *will be* (*be*) enough room for a bigger one in my new bedroom.
4. I'm sure I *won't give away* (*not give away*) my cat because she *'ll be* (*be*) my only friend for a long time!

6 Lauren's worries about Cornwall (→ p. 65/ex. 3)

a) *Lauren is thinking about her new home. Put in the words in the correct order.*

1. my school • miles away? • be • will Will my school be miles away?
2. there? • will • new friends • find • I Will I find new friends there?
3. a rap club? • will • be • there Will there be a rap club?
4. Nyla • will • in Cornwall? • me • visit Will Nyla visit me in Cornwall?

b) *Imagine you have to move away. Who or what will you miss most? Write two sentences.* (Lösungsvorschlag)

I will miss my friends. I will also miss my football club.

7 What will happen next? (→ p. 65/ex. 3)

Look at the photos. What do you think will happen next?

1

2

3

1. I think the dog will catch the ball.
2. I think it will rain soon.
3. I think the cat will eat the mouse.

8 What can they ask? (→ p. 65/ex. 4)

What can the people ask in these situations? Make questions with 'Shall I' … or 'Shall we' … .

1

carry

2

open

3

feed

1. Shall I carry the bags for you?
2. Shall I open the door for you?
3. Shall we feed the cat?

9 If … (→ p. 66/ex. 1)

Match the sentences and fill in the correct forms of the verbs.

1. If I learn a lot for the test,	we *'ll walk* (walk) into town.
2. If you like action films,	you *'ll enjoy* (enjoy) Spiderman 3.
3. If my dad doesn't have to work late,	I *won't get* (not get) a good mark.
4. If the rain doesn't stop,	I *won't go* (not go) outside.
5. If we don't find the car keys,	it *won't eat* (not eat) much cat food.
6. If I don't work harder for Maths,	I *'ll get* (get) a good mark.
7. If a cat catches a lot of mice,	we *'ll go* (go) to the cinema

10 What will happen if … (→ p. 66/ex. 2)

Put in the correct forms of the verbs.

1. If Carrie *misses* (miss) her favourite TV programme, she *won't be* (not be) happy for the rest of the evening.
2. If you *don't like* (not like) tomatoes, you *won't like* (not like) this salad.
3. If my sister *doesn't help* (not help) me in the kitchen, I *'ll tell* (tell) my mum.
4. If my favourite actor *plays* (play) in a new film, I *'ll buy* (buy) the DVD.
5. If I *get* (get) a good mark in my next English test, my dad *will give* (give) me £5.
6. If I *move* (move) to another town, I hope you *'ll send* (send) me lots of e-mails.

11 What will you do if … (→ p. 66/ex. 2) *(Lösungsvorschlag)*

Complete the sentences. Use your own ideas.

1. If I get £20 for my birthday, *I'll buy a new computer game.*
2. If the weather is fine this afternoon, *I'll go outside.*
3. If I don't get any homework today, *I'll play football with my friends.*
4. If you don't change your clothes for a week, *you'll smell terrible.*
5. If we go away on holiday next summer, *I'll have lots of fun.*
6. If you eat too much chocolate, *you'll be sick.*

12 Lauren's letter (→ p. 67/ex. 3)

Fill in the correct pronoun.

Dear Nyla,

We (We/Our/Us) are now in Cornwall and the house is really nice. It (It/Its) is much bigger than our old one and I really like my (I/me/my) new room. Dad likes his (he/him/his) new job and he (he/him/his) gets more money than in London. Mum likes her (she/her) garden and she spends a lot of time in it (it/its). The neighbours are very nice. They (They/Them/Their) have got a big dog. Her (She/Her) name is Yellow and, of course, Buffy hates her (she/her)! I (I/Me/My) have met some nice girls at school but I (I/me/my) still miss you (you/your) all very much! Please write soon!

Love, Lauren

13 Hello (→ p. 67/ex. 4)

Complete the dialogues with the correct reflexive pronouns.

1. Nyla: I wanted to speak French during my holidays in France so I taught myself French.
   Lauren: You taught yourself French? That's cool! Isn't that very difficult?
   Nyla: The French book which I used is easy to understand. It explains itself. You can teach yourself with it.

2. Carrie and Nyla: We really enjoyed ourselves at your goodbye party.
   Lauren: Oh, that's great. But did the others enjoy themselves as well?
   Carrie and Nyla: We think so. But Josh was so sad that you moved to Cornwall. He didn't really enjoy himself at the party.

14 My own rap (→ p. 67/ex. 4) *(Lösungsvorschlag)*

Look at page 67 in your book and write your own rap about yesterday. Read it to the class.

I got up on *Monday and washed myself.*

Then I went to the bedroom and dressed myself.

I went to school and didn't enjoy myself.

At home I went to the kitchen and fed myself.

15 Mediation and communication: At an English school (→ p. 69/ex. 2)

Work with a partner. You are exchange pupils at an English school. Make dialogues.

A

- frage, ob die Schule ein Volleyballteam hat

(Our school doesn't have a volleyball team but there is a football team.)

- frage nach dem Weg zur Cafeteria

(Yes, of course. I'll show you the way.)

- frage, wo du den Hausmeister findest

(The caretaker's office is next to the cafeteria)

- frage, wo du einen Schlüssel für dein Schließfach bekommst

(You can get a key from the secretary.)

- bedanke dich

(You're welcome!)

B

(Does your school have a volleyball team?)

- antworte, dass es kein Volleyballteam gibt, aber dass es ein Fußballteam gibt

(Can you show me the way to the cafeteria, please?)

- antworte, dass du gerne den Weg zeigst

(Where can I find the caretaker?)

- antworte, dass der Hausmeister sein Büro neben der Cafeteria hat

(Where can I get a key for my locker?)

- antworte, dass man einen Schlüssel bei der Sekretärin bekommen kann

(Thank you!)

- sage, dass du gerne geholfen hast

16 Mediation and communication: The British school system (→ p. 69/ex. 2)

Work with a partner. Look at the grid with the British school system and answer the questions in German.

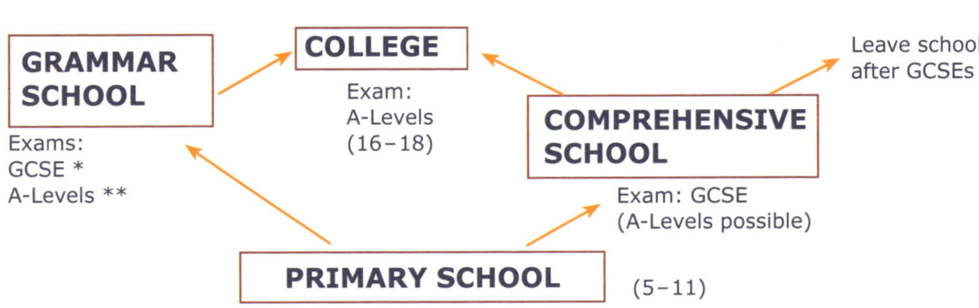

1. Wann beginnt die Schulpflicht in Großbritannien?
2. Wie lange geht dort die Grundschule?
3. Welche Prüfung kannst du mit 16 machen?
4. Wann kannst du die Schule verlassen?
5. Was sind 'A-Levels'?

17 Different words for the same message

(→ p. 68/ex. 1)

a) Look at these text messages. What do the short forms mean? Write down the full messages.

1. *I've got great news for you.*
2. *Are you coming to the party?*
3. *I can't see you today.*

b) *Read Lauren's e-mail. Use the short forms from the list and change it into a text message.*

ASAP – as soon as possible	GOIN2 – going to	PRT – party
B4N – bye for now	HRU – How are you?	R – are
Dur – Do you remember?	PCM – please call me	2NITE – tonight

Hi Nyla,

How are you? Do you remember Tom?
We are going to a party tonight!
Please call me as soon as possible!

Bye for now,
Lauren

Hi Nyla! HRU? Dur Tom? We R GOIN2 PRT 2NITE!
PCM ASAP! B4N, Lauren

18 Your own letter

(→ p. 68/ex. 2) *(Lösungsvorschlag)*

You have forgotten your grandma's birthday. Write a letter to her.

Dear Grandma,

I'm so sorry that I forgot your birthday. I had an accident with my bike and hurt my head. I can't even remember my name but Mum has given me a note with everything which is important.

I hope you had a nice birthday.

Love, ...

19 Let's listen: Strict parents? (→ p. 69/ex. 1)

Listen to the text again and look at the sentences. Who talks about which problem? Draw lines.

- We don't even do our homework together now.
- My parents argue all the time. I really need some advice.
- I have to be home by 10 o'clock but I want to stay out later, like my friends.
- My best friend has no time for me because she has now got a boyfriend.
- At school, my friends have lots to talk about but I have nothing to say.
- She spends all her time with her boyfriend and when I call she is always busy.

20 On the phone (→ p. 69/ex. 2) *(Lösungsvorschlag)*

a) *You want to go to the cinema with your friend. Use the phrases and write a telephone dialogue.*

You: *Hi, it's …*

Friend: *Hello!*

You: *Shall we go to the cinema tonight?*

Friend: *That's a great idea!*

You: *Shall we meet at the bus stop?*

Friend: *OK. See you then!*

Bye. •
Shall we … •
Hello, it's … speaking. •
That's a good idea! •
OK. See you then. •
Hi, it's …

b) *Think of your own message to leave on your friend's answerphone. Write it down and read it to your partner.*

Hello, it's … speaking. I'm sorry I can't go to the cinema with you. See you at school tomorrow. Bye!

21 Let's listen: Lauren's first day at school (→ p. 69/ex. 2)

It's Lauren's first day at her new school in Cornwall. Listen to the text. Which of these answers is correct?

1. Lauren is nervous because
   - a. she's looking in the mirror. [ ]
   - b. it's her first day at school. [x]
   - c. her mum is in the living-room. [ ]

2. How long must Lauren walk to school?
   - a. between 8 and 15 minutes. [ ]
   - b. about 1 hour and 20 minutes. [ ]
   - c. about 20 minutes. [x]

3. Lauren tells the girl that she
   - a. lives in Brighton Street. [ ]
   - b. lives in in the neighbourhood. [ ]
   - c. lives in Dayton Street. [x]

4. Lauren is happy because
   - a. she already knows Diane. [ ]
   - b. Myra is her age and she now has a friend. [x]
   - c. Diane is very friendly to her. [ ]

22 SKILLS: A new poem (→ p. 71/ex. 2) *(Lösungsvorschlag)*

a) *Read the poem. There are four parts of the poem. What are they about? Write one sentence for each part.*

1. The first part is about a bird which is *sitting in a tree and singing.*
2. The second part *is about a beautiful girl.*
3. *The third part is about a boy who is crying.*
4. *The fourth part is about a huge black cloud.*

b) *Look at the photo. Which part of the poem does it show? Find photos for the other parts of the poem and show them to the class.*

c) *Find a title for the poem:* *A normal day*

23 SKILLS: My own poem (→ p. 71/ex. 3)

a) *You can also make poems with names or other words. Each line can have one or more words. Look at these two poems:*

Blue
Eyes
Nice

Sun
Now
On
White

b) *Make your own poem. You can use your dictionary if it's hard to find the right words. Try to complete these first. Then make your own poem. Don't forget the picture!* *(individuelle Schülerlösung)*

People
Are dancing to
Rap songs
T *hey're*
Y *oung*

Laugh
In the sun
F *un*
E *very day*

24 School words (→ p. 72/ex. 1)

Write definitions for these words.

locker • cafeteria • Chemistry • library • teacher

1. A locker is a place where you can keep your things.
2. A cafeteria is a place where you can eat something.
3. Chemistry is a subject which you have at school.
4. A library is a place where you can borrow books.
5. A teacher is someone who teaches at school.

25 Word circle (→ p. 73/ex. 3)

Find all the words in the circle and mark them with different colours. Write down the nouns for the verbs.

speaker, action, sign, beginning, building,
catcher, choice, driver, ending, feeling, fishing,
travel, hate, smoke, help, interview, invitation,
life, meaning, note, joke, argument, organizer,
batter, paint, performance, play, fight, practise,
singer, suggestion, guard.

26 A crazy picture (→ p. 73/ex. 5)

Write down all the things which you can see in the picture.

TV, bookes, apple, computer, exercise
book, shelf, desk, poster, bed,
T-shirt, gloves, mp3 player, chocolate,
rucksack, pens, bottle of water, trousers,
shorts, envelopes, banana, sandwich,
glass

27 When Nyla and Carrie visit Lauren in Cornwall ... (→ p. 74/ex. 1)

Write down what Nyla and Carrie will do and what they won't do when they're in Cornwall.

Nyla and Carrie won't go to school. They will go to the beach.

They will play beach volleyball. They won't watch TV.

They won't do their homework. They will write postcards.

They will take photos. They won't play computer games.

28 Carrie's poetry slam (→ p. 74/ex. 2)

Carrie's friends are talking about the poetry slam in Bristol. They are making plans. Put in the correct forms of the verbs.

1. If there is ______ *(be)* a poetry slam in Bristol, Carrie will take ______ *(take)* part.
2. If she performs ______ *(perform)* in Bristol, we will watch ______ *(watch)* her.
3. If her performance is ______ *(be)* good, she will win ______ *(win)* the competition.
4. Carrie will be ______ *(be)* very sad if she doesn't win ______ *(not win)* the poetry slam.
5. If she wins ______ *(win)*, we will have ______ *(have)* a big party.

29 Reflexive pronouns (→ p. 75/ex. 3)

Put in the missing reflexive pronouns.

1. I normally repair my bike myself ______.
2. When I go out, my parents always say: "Look after yourself ______".
3. Josh washes himself ______ every morning.
4. Nyla and Carrie are old enough to look after themselves ______ when their parents are out.
5. Jane dresses herself ______ up for the party.
6. We enjoyed ourselves ______ at the party.
7. Can your cat feed itself ______?

1 Children at work – Great Britain and India (→ p. 76/ex. 4)

Hello! I'm Josh and I'm 14 years old. I need £200 because I want to buy a new bike. But I don't get much pocket money. That's why I've got a job. I work at a supermarket after school and on Saturdays. I would like to work more, but children in the U.K. should not work more than 12 hours a week in school time.

Hi, my name is Rashid and I'm 12 years old. My family is very poor. That's why I have to work. I don't have time to go to school because I work at least 15 hours a day. My family needs the money to buy food. I work for a company which makes car wheels. It's a very dangerous job and I'm sometimes scared when I'm at work, because there have been several accidents in the past few months and people have died.

a) *Read the texts and finish the sentences.*

1. Josh has got a job, because *he wants to buy a new bike.*
2. He works at *a supermarket after school and on Saturdays.*
3. Children in the UK *should not work more than 12 hours a week.*
4. Rashid works, because *his family is very poor.*
5. His family *needs the money to buy food.*
6. He can't go to school because *he has to work for a company which makes car wheels.*
7. Rashid is scared because *there have been several accidents and people have died.*

b) *What do you think about children who have jobs? Write a short text. The words in the box can help you.*

(Lösungsvorschlag)

In my opinion *children should have a job. If you have your own money, you can buy what you like. But I don't think it's right for children to work all time. I believe that they should go school, too. I think it's wrong for children to have dangerous jobs.*

In my opinion, … should … .
In my opinion, … shouldn't … .
I think that … .
I don't think that … .
I believe that … .
I don't believe that … .
I think it's right for … .
I think it's wrong for … .

c) *Read your text to the class and discuss it.*

2 A discussion (→ p. 77/ex. 5)

Your group has won 200 Euros in a competition at school. What do you want to do with the money? Discuss.

Unit 5 Screen shots

1 Bollywood film (→ p. 80/ex. 1)

Read the poem and fill in the correct words.

dramatic • grave • heroine • kiss • shot • thriller • tough • twice

This film is great. I think it's a *thriller*.
But is he really going to kill her?
I thought that she was the *heroine*.
The girl that they're all trying to win.
But suddenly the hero hears a *shot*
and there's a fire somewhere. He's getting hot.
This film is really very *dramatic*.
It's the kind of film I always pick.

The hero is great. He's very *tough*.
But will he really be good enough?
And at the end will he save his heroine from
an early *grave*?
And what was that? What did I miss?
I thought I saw … . Did I see them *kiss*?
Oh. Look at that! Isn't that nice?
He kissed her once and she kissed him *twice*.

2 Which programmes do you watch? (→ p. 81/ex. 3)

a) *What kind of TV programmes or films are these teenagers talking about?*

1. Oh, I really like it. It's so funny. My dad is just like the one on TV. He often does stupid things, too. The voices and the pictures are so good – you don't need to see real actors.
   cartoon

2. I love that programme. It's funny and sometimes it's scary. They meet aliens and I like it when they travel back in time. I'd like to do that, too.
   science fiction

3. Oh, I love them. And the ones about animals are the best. I think they are really interesting. I mean, did you know that the lion is the second largest cat, after the tiger? And that lions sleep 20 hours a day?
   documentary

4. The film was great. I laughed all the time and the story was good. It was about a detective who had to find a burglar, but the detective was just too stupid. It wasn't really a detective story, of course – it was too funny.
   comedy

b) *Find an example for each kind of programme on German TV.* (Lösungsvorschlag)

1. *The Simpsons*
2. *Stargate*
3. *Abenteuer Leben*
4. *Bullyparade*

c) *Write about your favourite programme in your exercise book. Let your partner guess what kind of programme it is.* (individuelle Schülerlösung)

3 What's that? (→ p. 82/ex. 1)

What can you see in the pictures? Look at the TV programme in your book on page 82. Which programme is it?

1

patient
ER

2
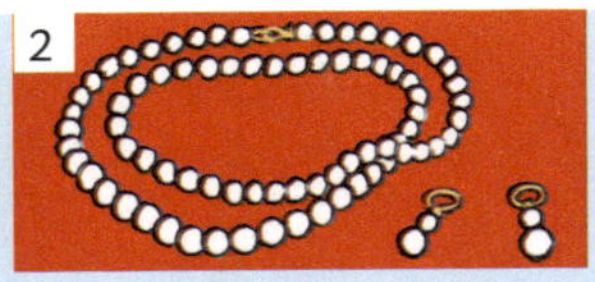
jewellery
Diamond Hotel

3

doctor
Pet Tips

4

cook
Ready Steady Cook

5

alien
My parents are Aliens

6

hound
Sherlock Holmes

7

singer
Top of the Pops

8

game show host
Countdown

4 Pet Tips (→ p. 82/ex. 2)

Put a circle around the correct word.

Dr Lion: Do you have some • any pets?
Mark: No, I had some • any mice but then my brother got a cat and …
Sue: I have a dog and he doesn't eat some • any pet food. What can I give him?
Dr Lion: You can give him some • any of your food. Give him some • any meat and vegetables.
Sue: I don't eat some • any vegetables.
Ben: I don't have some • any pets but I have a sister and she never does what I want her to do.
Dr Lion: Well, I'm sorry. I can't give you some • any help there.

5 Countdown (→ p. 82/ex. 2)

This TV show is a letter game. In each round the players get some letters and each player tries to make a word with them. Look at these groups of letters. Which letters are there? Which aren't there? Write sentences with 'some' and 'any'. Try to make a word with the letters.

1. ECESRN
There are some "E"s
but there aren't "A"s.
Word: screen

2. NECES
There are some "E"s
but there aren't any "B"s.
Word: scene

3. SSIK
There are some "S"s
but there aren't any "N"s.
Word: kiss

4. KCOO
There are some "O"s
but there aren't any "M"s.
Word: cook

6 Where's Rob? (→ p. 83/ex. 4)

PC Burns is talking to Rob's mum. Put in words with 'some' and 'any'.

somewhere • anywhere	something • anything	somebody • anybody

PC Burns: I'd like to see Rob's bedroom. Maybe he has left *something* which tells us where he has gone.

Mrs Pearl: Oh, of course. I can show you his bedroom. But I'm sure you won't find *anything* there.

PC Burns: What's this? A pink shopping bag …

Mrs Pearl: I've never seen this bag before. I think *somebody* has left it in Rob's room. But who?

PC Burns: Has *anybody* been in Rob's room since yesterday?

Mrs Pearl: No! But I know there is a shop *somewhere* in Avondale where you get these bags. Or can you get them *anywhere* else?

PC Burns: I'll find out and talk to the shop assistant.

7 An alien on holiday (→ p. 83/ex. 4)

An alien is showing photos from his holiday to a friend. Complete his friend's questions and write down what he answers. Use 'some' or 'any' or words with 'some' and 'any'.

Did you go *anywhere* nice on holiday?

Yes, I went to Earth[1]. Look here are *some* photos. Look at that! That boy's sitting on *something* which you can ride. It's called a bike. People ride them when they want to go *somewhere*. And look at this photo. That was funny. They're all learning *something*. They're listening to *somebody* who is called a teacher. They have to stay there all day and can't go *anywhere* nice.

[1] Earth [ɜːθ] – *Erde*

8 Inspector I. Newitt (→ p. 84/ex. 1)

Before he became a police inspector, I. Newitt worked in a rescue team. Read his story about the rescue of a young man and fill in the past progressive.

"It was a horrible day. The wind was blowing (*to blow*) and the waves were pushing (*to push*) the boats towards the beach and the cliffs. But it wasn't raining (*not rain*) and some people were sitting (*to sit*) on the beach. Mr and Mrs Taylor were watching (*to watch*) their son who was surfing (*to surf*). Then they went to buy some ice-cream. When they looked at the water again, their son had disappeared. They were scared and called us on their mobile. Ten minutes later we were sitting (*to sit*) in our boat near the cliffs. It was very dangerous. Suddenly we saw their son. He was sitting (*to sit*) on the cliff with a girl. He had left the water while his parents had bought their ice-creams. I was so angry about that I left the rescue team and became a policeman."

9 The inspector's son (→ p. 84/ex. 1)

Inspector Newitt's son also wants to become an inspector when he is old enough. He wants to know everything about his dad's work. What did he ask his dad when he came back from Diamond Hotel? Write questions in the past progressive.

1. what • you • do • at 9 o'clock? What were you doing at 9 o'clock?
2. the jewellery • miss? Was the jewellery missing?
3. you • talk • the suspects? Were you talking to the suspect?
4. who • you • talk to • on the phone? Who were you talking to on the phone?

10 Inspector Newitt's notes (→ p. 82/ex. 2)

When Inspector I. Newitt comes home, he writes notes about what he has found out at the hotel. Look at his notes and write sentences. Use the past progressive.

jewellery not lie in safe • suspects not do what they told me • manager's girfriend not answer her phone • light in room no. 12 not work

1. The jewellery wasn't lying in the safe.
2. The suspects weren't doing what they told me.
3. The manager's girlfriend wasn't answering her phone.
4. The light in room no. 12 wasn't working.

11 Kate's favourite soap (→ p. 85/ex. 3)

Kate watches her favourite soap every day. Yesterday something funny happened. Read the text and put in the simple past or the past progressive.

When I came *(to come)* home yesterday, my mum and dad were working *(to work)* in the garden. Great! I could watch my favourite soap without them in the living room. I was sitting *(to sit)* on the sofa when the soap started *(to start)*. Alice and Jim, two of the stars, were eating *(to eat)* in the kitchen when there was *(to be)* a knock on the door. But they didn't open the door. When Alice left *(to leave)* the kitchen, the phone was ringing *(to ring)*.

But they didn't answer it. I was thinking *(to think)* that something was wrong on TV when I heard *(to hear)* a knock on the window – my window. It was my mum and dad. I had locked the door and they couldn't come into the house. They had knocked on the door and then phoned me. How embarrassing! When I opened *(to open)* the door, they were laughing *(to laugh)* at me.

12 A thriller? (→ p. 85/ex. 4)

What was happening? Look at the pictures and use the words to make sentences with 'while'.

1. While Kate was waiting, two teenagers were breaking into Kate's house.
2. While she was sitting on the bus, they were looking for a knife.
3. While she was walking home, they were hiding in the living room.
4. While they were singing "Happy Birthday", she was smiling happily.

13 SKILLS: Dictionary work (→ p. 86/ex. 1)

a) *Look up these words in a dictionary. Then read the text on page 86 again and write down the correct meaning.*

1. to turn sich umdrehen
2. hard heftig
3. to bury begraben

b) *Look up these words in a dictionary and write down their plurals.*

1. wife wives
2. tooth teeth
3. wolf wolves

14 SKILLS: New words (→ p. 86/ex. 1)

Match the pictures with the sentences and write down the German meanings of the underlined words.

1. Gelert's death was very sad. Picture D – Tod
2. It was shocking that the prince killed his dog, Gelert. Picture C — schockierend
3. Prince Llywelyn was very sad at his dog's burial. Picture F — Begräbnis
4. Llywelyn got a shock when he got home and the baby wasn't there. Picture B — Schock
5. Llywelyn liked to hunt. Picture A — jagen
6. Most people in the area heard of Gelert's bravery. Picture E — Mut

15 SKILLS: Inotation (→ p. 86/ex. 1)

Where does your voice go up or down in the sentences? Mark the sentences and read them to a partner.

1. Did you like the story? ↑
2. Do you know any other myths? ↑
3. It is a very old story. ↓
4. Have you ever been to Wales? ↑

16 Let's listen: An interesting role (→ p. 87/ex. 1)

Listen to the text and put a x in the correct box.

	Right	Wrong	not in the text
1. Amanda doesn't like interviews.	☐	☐	x
2. She was in New York when she got the part.	☐	x	☐
3. Amanda has acted in many TV dramas in Britain.	x	☐	☐
4. The director helped her practise her lines.	☐	x	☐
5. She tells the reporter a secret.	x	☐	☐

17 Intonation: An interesting role (→ p. 87/ex. 1)

Do these sentences go up or down at the end? Mark the sentences and read them to your partner.

1. Everybody at the hotel was talking about it. ↓
2. Did you just make them up? ↑
3. Ah, so that helped you. ↓
4. Will we no longer see Amanda Willis in TV dramas? ↑

18 Let's listen: Myths (→ p. 87/ex. 3)

Listen to this radio interview. Put a x after the correct sentences.

1. Bedgelert is a Welsh village which got its name after a dog in a myth. x
2. Myths are never true stories. ☐
3. A man wanted a tattoo which said, "I am a very ugly man." ☐
4. A man once took off his helmet and his head fell in half. x
5. People usually hear myths from their friends. ☐

19 A poem: Films (→ p. 87/ex. 4)

a) *Fill in the missing words and put the sentences of the poem in the right order.*

cry | die | race | night | kiss | jump

A But the worst films are love films where all the stars _kiss_.
Those are films that I want to miss!

B Sometimes aliens come down from space.
That often means trouble for the human _race_.

C Some films are sad – you watch them and _cry_.
You know that the hero ist going to _die_.

D Some films have spies – they fight, run and _jump_.
When they crash their cars, there's a very big bump!

1	2	3	4	5
C	D	B	E	A

E And then there are ghost films – ghosts come out at _night_.
And give everybody an awful fright.

b) *What kinds of films do you like best? Why? Write in your exercise book.* (individuelle Schülerlösung)

20 Mediation and communication: A film quiz (→ p. 87/ex. 4)

Tell your partner in German what these films are about. Does he/she know the German title of the film?

A

The monsters live in Monstropolis and a lot of them work in the main power company Monsters, Inc. They go through doors into children's rooms and scare the children. But the monsters are also afraid of the children because they think that they are very dangerous. One day, the top scarer of Monsters, Inc. finds a small girl who has come through one of the doors. And now, he has got a problem.

Three years after the beginning of the Clone Wars, Jedi Knight Anakin Skywalker and Jedi Master Obi Wan Kenobi are still fighting. Anakin has nightmares in which his wife is dying. He wants to save her. But how will he do this? Will he really turn to the Dark Side?

Life in the sea can be really dangerous, especially when you are a tiny clown fish. And Marlin does everything to protect his only son Nemo. But on Nemo's first day of school, Marlin's nightmare comes true: Nemo disappears! And Marlin starts his dangerous journey into the open sea to find him … .

B

Captain Jack Sparrow is in trouble again. This time, Will Turner and Elizabeth Swann are looking for him, because the authorities will arrest them if they don't get Jack Sparrow. Will Jack escape again? And what does the scary captain of the Flying Dutchman want from Jack? Find out in the second part of the pirate adventure!

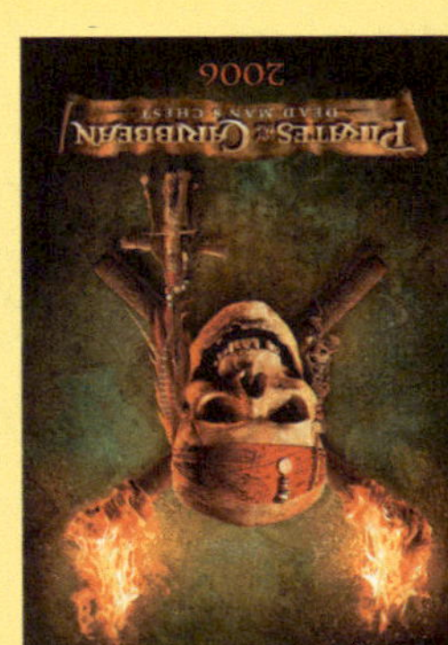

A terrorist called Le Chiffre needs money for his plans and organizes a poker game. But James Bond is also there. The game begins and there are not only cards in the game but the players also do dirty tricks. And what role is the Bond girl playing? Who will win the game?

What if the new Ice Age actually starts tomorrow? While scientist Jack warns the White House, his son Sam is in New York City. But a huge flood is coming and Jack travels to New York to save Sam. What will happen – to him, to his son, and to the whole planet?

21 The people in the story (→ p. 89/ex. 2)

a) *Look at the pictures of the people in the story 'The Hound of the Baskervilles'. Write the people's names under the pictures.*

1. Mr Stapleton

2. Dr Watson

3. Sir Charles Baskerville

4. Barrymore

5. Sherlock Holmes

b) *Describe the people. Write one sentence for each picture.* (Lösungsvorschlag)

1. Mr Stapleton has fair hair. He wears a white coat like a scientist.
2. Dr Watson is Sherlock Holmes's assistant.
3. Sir Charles Baskerville is the inheritor of Baskerville Hall.
4. Barrymore is a servant at Baskerville Hall. He has a black beard.
5. Sherlock Holmes is a famous detective.

22 What happened? (→ p. 91/ex. 5)

Put these events in the correct order.

3	Sherlock Holmes, Dr Watson and Sir Henry arrive on Dartmoor.
5	The Hound of the Baskervilles is coming to get Sir Henry.
2	Sir Henry visits Sherlock Holmes and his assistant, Dr Watson, at 221b Baker Street, London.
6	The policemen arrest Mr Stapleton.
1	Sir Henry loses a second boot.
4	Mr Stapleton invites them to supper.

23 A different ending (→ p. 91/ex. 7) (Lösungsvorschlag)

a) *Choose one of the two pictures on page 91 which show a different ending. Write the new ending.*

The hound jumped at Sir Charles Baskerville but Mr Stapleton was at the window. He had a gun and killed the hound. Now it was safe again.

b) *Read your new ending to the class.*

24 A poem: I love TV (→ p. 92/ex. 1) *(Lösungsvorschlag)*

Read the peom. Put circles around the rhyming words. Find another word for each rhyme.

I love TV. I love all the (series) *secretaries*
And films and (documentaries). *marries*

I cry when a dog or some other (pet) *bet*
dies on a docu soap and I also (get) *let*

scared when I watch some horrible (hound) *round*
which kills people without a (sound). *pound*

And when I watch a soap with a (lad) *mad*
who runs away because he's (sad). *bad*

I worry about the (runaway) *say*
Though I know he'll come back one (day). *May*

And then I feel hungry when a good (cook) *look*
makes a meal without a (book). *took*

And, yes, I like talk shows with a good (host) *ghost*
But you know what I love (most)? *post*

Science fiction films with little green (men) *pen*
where the heroine is an (alien). *when*

25 A puzzle (→ p. 92/ex. 3)

a) *Answer the questions and fill in the words.*

1. not very often
2. a funny programme or film
3. when two mouths touch
4. not very big and not very small
5. this makes lots of something
6. two times
7. dead people lie in these
8. blond; not dark
9. a person who watches TV
10. a film where the actors sing
11. the opposite of weak
12. a film which is very scary
13. you watch them on TV
14. a girl hero

1. *SEL**D**OM*
2. *C**O**MEDY*
3. *KISS*
4. *AVERAGE*
5. *I**N**DUSTR**Y***
6. *TWI**C**E*
7. *GRAVE*
8. *F**A**IR*
9. *VIEWE**R***
10. *M**U**SICAL*
11. *TOUGH*
12. ***T**HRILLER*
13. *PROGRA**M**ME*
14. *HEROIN**E***

b) *Which word do you get?*

documentary

26 Odd one out (→ p. 93/ex. 4)

Which of these is the odd one out?

brave	assistant	servant (Diener)	patient
shocked	actor	beard (Bart)	scientist (Wissensch…)
blood	heroine	nephew (Neffe)	cook
dead	screen	lad	director
blood	*screen*	*beard*	*patient*

27 Ready steady cook for wizards (→ p. 94/ex. 2)

Complete these sentences with 'some', 'any' or words with 'some' and 'any'.

Wizzy: Would anybody ______ like to try this?

Ozzy: Well, I've never seen anything ______ that looks so interesting. But I think it just needs something ______ sweet.

Wizzy: I know there were some ______ dogs' legs on the table but I can't find them anywhere ______.

Ozzy: I don't have any dog's legs but you can have some ______ of my cat's ears if you want.

Wizzy: Oh, thank you! It's always good when there is somebody ______ who helps you.

28 A broken arm (→ p. 95/ex. 3)

Choose the correct verb and fill in the correct form of the past progressive.

sit | ride | talk | not look | do | hurt | play

Sue: So what were ______ you doing ______?

Kate: We were riding ______ through the park on our bikes and I wasn't looking ______ at the path. A boy was playing ______ football and he ran after the ball and onto the path. I rode into him and we both had to go to hospital. It was so nice.

Sue: Nice? But your arm was hurting ______ because it was broken!

Kate: Yes, but while we were sitting ______ next to each other, we were talking ______ and … .

29 Sports special – what went wrong? (→ p. 95/ex. 3)

Fill in the correct forms of the verbs.

1. A man was playing ______ *(play)* basketball when his shorts fell down ______ *(fall down)*.
2. Some runners were running ______ *(run)* a race when they got lost ______ *(get lost)*.
3. When the referee got ______ *(get)* knocked out, he wasn't watching ______ *(not watch)* the ball.

1 Writing a letter to a magazine (→ p. 97/ex. 3) *(individuelle Schülerlösung)*

Look at page 97 again and write your own letter to the magazine.

A Address with postcode
B Date
C You start like this
D First word with capital letter
E Why you are writing
F A new paragraph for each new idea
G Comments about the article
H Closing words
I Saying 'goodbye'
J Your name

(A)

(B)

(C)

(D)

(E)

(F)

(G)

(H)

(I)

(J)

Meine Lernbiografie 3

Jetzt hast du alle fünf Units bearbeitet. Male zu jedem Satz einen Smiley in der entsprechenden Farbe. Was war gut, und was möchtest du ändern? Frage auch deinen Lehrer/deine Lehrerin, ob er/sie dir Tipps geben kann.

Was ich alles kann!

sehr gut · gut · muss ich noch üben

			Übung im ... Seite/Übung
Hören	Ich kann Hörtexten einzelne Informationen entnehmen und Fragen zum Gehörten beantworten.		Schülerbuch S. 62/2, S. 69/1, 2, S. 87/1, 2 Workbook S. 49/19, S. 61/16, 18
	Ich verstehe auch längere Hörtexte und kann Teile daraus wiedergeben.		Schülerbuch S. 62/2 b), S. 69/1, 2 Workbook S. 49/21
Sprechen	Ich kann über Probleme sprechen.		Schülerbuch S. 63/4 Workbook S. 43/1
	Ich kann ein Foto beschreiben.		Schülerbuch S. 62/1 Workbook S. 45/7, S. 52/26
	Ich kann Sätze im *will-future* bilden.		Schülerbuch S. 65/2, 3 Workbook S. 44/4, 5, S. 45/6, 7
	Ich kann *if*-Sätze bilden.		Schülerbuch S. 66/1, 2 Workbook S. 46/9, 10, 11
	Ich kann das britische Schulsystem erklären und mit dem deutschen vergleichen.		Schülerbuch S. 67/5 Workbook S. 48/16
	Ich kann ein Gedicht oder einen Text ausdrucksstark vorlesen.		Schülerbuch S. 71/3, S. 86/1 Workbook S. 51/22, 23
	Ich kann meine eigene Meinung ausdrücken und in der Gruppe über ein Thema diskutieren.		Schülerbuch S. 77/3, 4, 5 Workbook S. 54/1, 2
	Ich kann über Filme sprechen und Filminhalte auf Deutsch wiedergeben.		Schülerbuch S. 80/1, S. 81/4 Workbook S. 62/20
	Ich kann Sätze mit *some* und *any* und ihren Zusammensetzungen bilden.		Schülerbuch S. 83/3, 4 Workbook S. 56/3, 4, 5, S. 57/6, 7
	Ich kann mit dem *past progressive* ausdrücken, wenn in der Vergangenheit gerade etwas passiert ist.		Schülerbuch S. 84/3, 4 Workbook S. 58/8, 9, 10, S. 59/11, 12
Lesen	Ich kann längere Geschichten lesen und verstehen.		Schülerbuch S. 89/2, S. 91/3, 4
	Ich kann Einzelheiten aus Texten herausfinden und Aufgaben dazu lösen.		Schülerbuch S. 91/5, 6 Workbook S. 63/21, 22

	Ich kann Gedichte lesen und interpretieren.		Schülerbuch S. 71/1, 2 Workbook S. 51/22, 23
Schreiben	Ich kann über Erlebtes oder Erfundenes schreiben.		Schülerbuch S. 65/5, S. 83/5, S. 85/5 Workbook S. 63/23
	Ich kann eine E-Mail schreiben.		Schülerbuch S. 66/2 Workbook S. 49/17
	Ich kann einen Tagebucheintrag, eine sms, eine Notiz und/oder einen Brief schreiben.		Schülerbuch S. 68/1, 2 Workbook S. 49/17, 18
	Ich kann einen Zeitungsbericht schreiben.		Schülerbuch S. 91/7
	Ich kann einen Leserbrief schreiben.		Schülerbuch S. 97/2, 3 Workbook S. 66/1

Was ich noch besser machen kann!

Hast du deine Lernziele aus der Lernbiografie 2 erreicht? Was war gut, und was möchtest du ändern? Damit du deine guten Vorsätze nicht vergisst, schreib sie doch einfach wieder auf.

Konntest du die Ziele, die du dir nach Unit 3 gesetzt hast, erreichen? Was konntest du verbessern?

____

Welche Schwierigkeiten tauchten beim Lernen auf? Wie konntest du sie überwinden?

____

____

Worauf bist du in dieser Lerneinheit besonders stolz?

____

Welche Arbeiten aus deinem Folder zeigen besonders gut, was du erreichst hast und/oder wo du dich verbessert hast?

____

Was möchtest du in Zukunft noch stärker üben?

____

Tipps von deinem Lehrer/deiner Lehrerin:

____

____

Datum: ______________ Unterschrift: ______________________________

ÜBERSICHT

SKILLS

Communication Skills	Schülerbuch S. 118 – 121
Dictionary Skills	Schülerbuch S. 22, Workbook S. 14
Discussion Skills • Rules for a discussion	 Schülerbuch S. 77, Workbook S. 54
Grammar Skills	Schülerbuch S. 122
Group Skills • A play project	Schülerbuch S. 111
Language Skills • Adverts	Schülerbuch S. 59, Workbook S. 40
Picture Skills • Getting information from pictures	Schülerbuch S. 100
Poetry Skills • Picture Language	Schülerbuch S. 71, Workbook S. 51
Presentation Skills • Preparing a talk • Giving a talk • Presenting a poem	 Schülerbuch S. 14, Workbook S. 8 Schülerbuch S. 14, Workbook S. 8 Schülerbuch S. 71, Workbook S. 51
Reading Skills • Skimming • Expressive reading	Schülerbuch S. 32, S. 100, Workbook S. 22 Schülerbuch S. 86, Workbook S. 60
Speaking Skills • Being polite	Schülerbuch S. 50, Workbook S. 34
Text Skills • Keeping a reader's diary • Recognizing a play	Schülerbuch S. 101 Schülerbuch S. 110
Writing Skills • Writing a story • Tips for a summary • Designing adverts • Personal writing • Planning a letter • Spelling	 Schülerbuch S. 40, Workbook S. 28 Schülerbuch S. 53, Workbook S. 37 Schülerbuch S. 59, Workbook S. 40 Schülerbuch S. 68, Workbook S. 49 Schülerbuch S. 97, Workbook S. 66 Schülerbuch S. 101

Workbook-Hörverstehenstexte

Unit 1 S. 9/ex. 17 Let's listen: Is it important to win?

Jenny: Look, you two. There's Ben.
Tracy: Oh yes. Let's go and talk to him.
Mark: Hi, Ben!
Ben: Oh, hello.
Jenny: Hey, what's wrong?
Ben: I'm fed up. I lost my tennis match this afternoon.
Mark: Oh, bad luck. But it isn't so important to win all the time.
Ben: Yes, it is! Of course it's important when you want to be the best.
Jenny: You're right, Ben. I don't play tennis, but I do the long jump. It's important to me to win, too.
Tracy: But the fact is, not everybody can win. So why get fed up? It's silly.
Mark: You're right, Tracy. Sport is for fun. Even when you lose, you can enjoy it.
Ben: Don't be silly! You look like an idiot when you lose.
Mark: No, you don't.
Jenny: But it's much cooler to win!
Ben: That's what I think, too, Jenny. Everybody loves the person who wins.
Mark: Well, I don't like people just because they're good at sport. There are much more important things than sport.
Tracy: You're right, Mark! And my father says it's good to lose sometimes.
Jenny: What?! Good to lose?!
Tracy: Yes. He says it's an important lesson in life to learn how to lose.
Ben: I don't think that's true. It's better to learn how to win.
Jenny: Ben is right. When you win it makes you happy. Doesn't everybody want to be happy?
Tracy: But my father says –
Mark: Oh, forget your father, Tracy! Come on, let's all go to my house and watch …

Unit 2 S. 23/ex. 15 Let's listen: Up and down

1. This is a really fantastic city. There's so much to see and do.
2. Tomorrow it will be sunny in the morning and wet in the afternoon.
3. Please bring us a pizza, the spaghetti and a lemonade.
4. I know you like old ships, so let's visit the Cutty Sark .
5. After we've been to the Tower, we can come back to Westminster by boat.

Unit 2 S. 23/ex. 17 Let's listen: Opinions about London

A: Excuse me. I'm doing a survey about London. I'm trying to find out what visitors think is good or bad. So my first question is - are you a visitor?
B: Yes, I'm from Italy. I arrived in London last week and I'm having a very good time.
A: I'm happy to hear you're enjoying your visit! What do you like about London?
B: Well, there are so many things to see and do. It's hard to choose where to go first! But I think the museums a great. There are lots of different ones, and they are all very interesting - even if some of them aren't cheap.
A: Do you think prices are high here?
B: Oh yes, everything is very expensive. I've spent a lot of money in the last few days. I don't want to think how much I've spent!
A: What about London shops? What do you think about them?
B: Everything is different here in Britain. In Italy shops are not open in the early afternoon. And in the evening British shops close earlier. But it's OK. What's funny about shops here is that people wait in queues every where. You don't find that in Italy.
A: Do you think the restaurants in London are OK?
B: Well, people say the food in England is terrible. But I don't think that's true. I've had some good meals in London. Chinese. Indian. Italian. I don't think there are many English restaurants in London!
A: The sandwich shops are English!
B: Oh yes, and the sandwiches are very good. I often buy them for lunch because it's cheaper. And you're never far from a park. It's nice to eat outside. In Italy people try to be outside as much as they can. They talk and laugh in the streets together.
A: Well, but the streets are never empty here.
B: Yes, that's right. But everything is faster here. I think people don't have so much time for each other. But I don't want to say that British people have no time. If you need help or ask for the way, they always have time for you and are very polite.

Unit 3 S. 35/ex. 18 Let's listen: Where's Susi?

Kevin: Can we go to the beach now Mum, I'm bored?
Mum: Not until we've bought Susi a rubber ring. Susi? Where is that girl now?
Kevin: I don't know where the little goblin is.
Mum: Kevin! Don't talk about your little sister like that. Now, she can't be far. Come on!
Er … excuse me, I'm sorry to bother you, but have you seen a little girl? She's got brown hair and she's wearing a red t-shirt.
Man: Um, no, sorry, I'm just a customer here. Have you lost her? Would you like me to help you look for her?
Mum: No, no, it's ok. She really can't be far. Come on Kevin.
Kevin: Maybe a leprechaun took her, Mum. But I don't think we're that lucky.
Mum: This is no time for your silly jokes Kevin. Now help me to look for her!
Kevin: O-K. Look, there's a shop assistant, I'll ask her. Um, excuse me. Could you help us please?
Shop ass: Yes, of course. What are you looking for?
Kevin: My sister.
Shop ass: Oh, I see, well … er … could you tell me what she looks like?
Kevin: Well, she's got a face like a gob …
Mum: I'll answer that question Kevin. She's 5, brown hair, red T-shirt, I don't know how I could have lost her.
Shop ass: Don't worry. I am sure we'll find her.
loudspeaker: Excuse me ladies and gentlemen. We have found a little girl who's lost. She's wearing a red T-shirt and jeans. What's your name little girl?
Susi: Susi.
loudspeaker: Could little Susi's Mum or Dad come to the information desk please, near the entrance. Susi's waiting for you. Thank you.
Shop ass: There you are. See, I told you not to worry.
Mum: Oh, thank God for that. Thank you very much. Let's go Kevin.
Kevin: Too, bad. Maybe I can do something to the rubber ring.
Mum: What did you say Kevin?
Kevin: I said, are we still going to get a rubber ring, Mum?
Mum: Yes, but let's get Susi first!

Unit 4 S. 50/ex. 21 Let's listen: Lauren's first day at schol

"Well Buffy, today's the day, so wish me luck."
Lauren put her cat down on the bed and turned to look in the mirror. The dark purple Kingsdale jacket and grey skirt looked really nice. Lauren picked up her new school rucksack and walked into the living-room.
"Bye, Mum".
Lauren was nervous again.
"Don't worry, dear, you'll be fine." Lauren's mother smiled and opened the front door. "It's normal to feel nervous on your first day at a new school. But I'm sure everything will be OK.
Kingsdale Comprehensive was not too far from Lauren's house and it only took her about 20 minutes to walk there. It was 8:15 now. She didn't want to be too early, so she walked around the playground and looked for a place to sit. A house across the street had a low wall in front of it. Lauren walked over and sat down. Just then a girl in Kingsdale school uniform came out of the house and walked down the path towards Lauren.
"Hi," she said. She smiled at Lauren. "Are you new around here?"
Lauren smiled back. "Yes, we moved here from Brighton two weeks ago. I live in Dayton Street."
"Dayton Street? That's where my friend Diane lives. She comes to my house every morning so we can walk to school together."
The girl sat down next to Lauren.
"By the way, my name is Myra. I'm in year 7."
"I'm Lauren, Lauren Granger, and I'm in year 7, too." Lauren said.
"Hey, look! Here comes Diane."
Myra got up and waved to her friend.
"We'll show you around school, Lauren, and you can meet our friends. I think you'll like it here."
"I'm sure I will, Myra." Lauren smiled and said to herself, "Maybe living here won't be so bad."

Unit 5 S.61/ex. 18 Let's listen: Myths

Expert: We all know some myths, like the one about the Welsh prince, Llywelyn, who killed his dog Gelert. The story is very old and the Welsh village, Bedgelert, got its name after the dog but we still don't know if it's true of not. It's a story. And we've had the same myths for hundreds or thousands of years but today we also have myths.

Interviewer: Can you give us an example?

Expert: Well, they're stories that lots of people have heard but they don't really know if they are true or not. We all hear the stories from a friend who knows somebody who was there or who it happened to. But we never meet the person who was there. What's interesting is that you hear the same stories in different countries.

Interviewer: Well, can you tell us a few?

Expert: Yes, of course. There's the one about the man who wanted a tattoo in Chinese which said, "Love is everything." A Chinese man did the tattoo for him and he was very proud of it until a few weeks later he went to a Chinese restaurant.

Interviewer: Oh no. Let me guess. It didn't say "Love is everything"?

Expert: No, it said, "I am stupid".

Interviewer: Oh no. And that really happened?

Expert: Well, we don't know. We have heard the same story in England, Germany and France. And have you ever heard the story about the man who had an accident on his bike? He didn't feel too bad but when he took off his helmet, his head fell in half.

Interviewer: Ugh. That's horrible.

Expert: Yes. And that really couldn't happen but many people know somebody who knows somebody who rode a bike ...

Interviewer: Oh, OK. Yes, I understand now. And how do they start?

Expert: Well, we don't really know. What we do know is how they are passed around, for example, by e-mail and by phone. Stories travel much faster than they did hundreds and thousands of years ago.

Orange **Line 3** Erweiterungskurs

Inhaltsverzeichnis der CD zum Hörverstehen

Track	Workbook Seite	Übung	Text/Übungstitel
1	9	16 (Unit 1)	Let's listen: At the match
2	9	17 (Unit 1)	Let's listen: Is it important to win?
3	23	15 (Unit 2)	Let's listen: Up and down
4	23	16 (Unit 2)	Let's listen: Could I have your attention, please?
5	23	17 (Unit 2)	Let's listen: Opinions about London
6	35	16 (Unit 3)	Let's listen: Your passport, please!
7	35	18 (Unit 3)	Let's listen: Where's Susi?
8	50	19 (Unit 4)	Let's listen: Strict parents?
9	50	21 (Unit 4)	Let's listen: Lauren's first day at school
10	61	16 (Unit 5)	Let's listen: An interesting role
11	61	18 (Unit 5)	Let's listen: Myths

Gesamtspielzeit: 27'33"